Southern Living®
Cookbook
Library

The
Salads
Cookbook

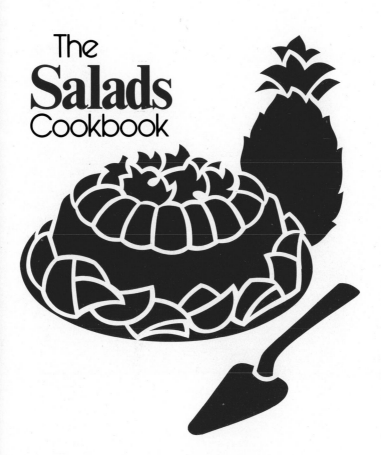

Copyright© 1979 Oxmoor House, Inc.
All rights reserved.
Library of Congress Catalog Number: 76–41145
ISBN: 0–8487–0330–8

Cover: *California Caesar Salad (page 81)*
Left: *Orange and Avocado Salad (page 104)*

contents

3

preface

What one category of food can fill virtually every role on your menu?

Southern Living homemakers know it's salads – presented as appetizers . . . side dishes . . . main dishes . . . buffet centerpieces . . . even desserts – salads enhance and blend with every food on every occasion.

Salads have much more to offer than mere versatility. They· are low in calories and high in nutritional values. They are low in cost of preparation – especially if you use seasonal fruits and vegetables and leftover meat and cheese. Yes, it's no wonder that salads are favorites among homemakers from Maryland to Texas.

It's not surprising that these enterprising women have turned their talents to the development of salad recipes using every imaginable fruit, vegetable, meat, seafood, and cheese – either alone or in combination. And to highlight their fabulous salads, southern homemakers have developed a variety of salad dressings.

Now, in one volume, the very best of these recipes are shared with you. You'll find recipes for special salad entrees . . . hearty meat salads . . . poultry salads . . . combination salads . . . and many more. You'll also find helpful charts giving the calorie values of foods most often included in salads. From our kitchens to yours, welcome to the wonderful world of salads – southern style!

Salads are only as good as the ingredients that go into them. For appetizing, picture-perfect salads, you'll want to buy the very best salad staples and store and prepare them as the experts do. When you follow this rule, you have taken a giant step toward serving your family and guests marvelous salads every time!

In this section, you'll find detailed information about buying, storing, and preparing salad staples used in almost every kind of salad — staples like lettuce, greens, and dressing ingredients. Information about buying, storing, and preparing ingredients used in certain kinds of salads — such as fruit — is featured in the chapter which focuses on that particular salad.

BUYING SALAD STAPLES

Buy the fresh salad produce you need after all your other marketing is done.

salads staples
BUYING, STORING, & PREPARING

If it is the first time you have visited a store, you'll want to check the cleanliness and temperature of the produce section. Are the counters clean? Is the temperature low? (Salad vegetables tend toward spoilage if the temperature is warm.) After a preliminary look around, notice how the produce is handled. Are stock boys cutting off the spoiled parts of vegetables and returning them to the counters? Is the fresher produce being placed beneath older stock? If the answer to either of these questions is yes, then don't buy. You will be getting inferior stock with few vitamin and mineral values intact.

Assuming that you have found a satisfactory produce section, check to see how the produce is wrapped. Ideally, you should be able to buy loose salad greens — so that you can see the entire vegetable and inspect it thoroughly. But you're apt to find most salad vegetables prepackaged. Some types of packaging — such as the so-called lattice packages — let you see all around the vegetable. But other kinds, especially those with a cardboard base, block the bottom of the vegetables from view. Result: you may get a poor head of lettuce or spoiled celery.

Consider local sources of garden vegetables. Large chain grocery stores may not have either the freshest or best-looking salad vegetables available. They must purchase from large suppliers, not local farmers who grow small quantities. But some of your locally owned grocery stores, curb markets, or even highway fruit and vegetable stands may be sources of that carefully tended, farm-fresh produce which is every homemaker's goal. Check your local resources — you may be pleasantly surprised at what is available!

Lettuce, whatever the type, is the foundation of your salad. It is cheapest in the spring and summer months when the supply is more plentiful. Head lettuce is available year-round, but during the spring and summer is almost twice as expensive as other varieties. Any lettuce should feel compact and heavy when you hold it in your hand. Open the leaves slightly to be sure there is no discoloration inside. Discard any lettuce that shows a tinge of rust — it is almost certain to be badly spoiled around the core.

Celery is another long-time favorite salad vegetable. It is in good supply year-round and is an economical buy. The greener the celery stalk, the more vitamins it contains. Celery stalks are very versatile — they are wonderful in salads and their leaves make a delicious flavor additive for soups and stews. Celery hearts are delicious but are suitable only for salads and may spoil easily.

Onions are a must for most salads. Avoid buying a sackful of onions unless you can use them quickly — they are highly susceptible to spoilage at room temperature. Don't buy onions with moisture at the neck, soft spots — certain signs of decay — or with new stems sprouting. In the springtime, green onions flood the produce market — sometimes selling for pennies a bunch. These tiny onions are excellent bargains — the tops can be used as a garnish and a flavoring for almost anything you cook. And the white onions add a sharp bite to your favorite salads.

Cucumbers are another popular salad vegetable and are particularly plentiful in late spring and early summer. The best cucumbers have a bright green color and are firm to the touch. Avoid cucumbers that are too large — they are probably tough-fleshed with hard seeds and make very poor eating. Cucumbers with withered ends or shriveled skin are bitter — and have poor taste.

To highlight the flavor of your carefully chosen salad staples, you'll want a good dressing. Oil and vinegar are the foundation of most dressings. The most popular *oil* for salad dressing is olive, and the finest olive oil is that know as "virgin" (the first pressing of the olive) from France. Thrifty home-makers use equal parts of olive and vegetable oil — they get the olive oil's inimitable flavor but at a fraction of the cost.

Wine vinegar — red or white — is most often used in salad dressings. How-ever, American cider vinegar or one of the herb-flavored vinegars will do as well.

STORING SALAD STAPLES

When you have bought all the salad vegetables you need to prepare a really great salad — how do you store them to retain that crisp, fresh flavor so important to successful salad making? As soon as you get home, take the lettuce out of the wrapping paper and wash thoroughly under cold, running water. For this step, the kitchen device known as a French basket is nice to have. This utensil is an open wire basket with a handle which is hung over the faucet. Water runs into the basket through the vegetables and out the holes — and the vegetables remain undisturbed.

After washing the lettuce thoroughly, cut off the stem end coring about one inch into the lettuce head. Separate the leaves and drain them. Romaine, escarole, and other firm lettuces can be separated after washing.

The more fragile lettuces — Boston, Bibb, field, etc. — should be pulled apart first, then washed by gently floating on cool water. Set the washed leaves on a dish towel or paper toweling and let them dry in the air.

Once your lettuce has been washed and dried, place it in a clean dish towel or plastic bag and put the wrapped lettuce in the vegetable crisper. If you are going to use the lettuce the same day, it may be torn into small pieces before placing in the refrigerator. Here's a clue if you're planning a really big salad. Wrap your lettuce in a pillow case. It's large enough to hold the amount you'll need and the torn lettuce will pour easily into your salad bowl. All lettuce needs at least half an hour in the refrigerator to crisp thoroughly.

Salad vegetables other than lettuce should be washed and placed in the vegetable crisper until you are ready to use them. If your crisper is less than half-full, wrap each vegetable or bunch of vegetables in a plastic bag — they will keep better than they would in the half-empty crisper.

Salad oils and vinegars should be stored in a cool, dry place. If oils are stored in the refrigerator, they are apt to cloud. About an hour before you are ready to use them, remove them and let them come to room temperature.

PREPARING SALAD STAPLES

For a *tossed salad,* the lettuce and other salad greens should be torn into bite-sized pieces or they may be cut with kitchen scissors. They should never be chopped or minced as only a torn or scissor-cut edge will hold the dressing properly. Vegetables other than lettuce should be cut in bite-sized pieces large enough so they retain their identity. If you use tomatoes in a tossed or green salad, be certain to drain them well and add them just before serving. Their juice tends to wilt the greens and dilute the dressing. Small cherry tomatoes, which are less juicy, are excellent for tossed salads.

Many hostesses enjoy mixing a tossed salad at the table. You may want to concoct your dressing at the table and add it to the salad you have made in advance. But if you would like to prepare both your dressing and your salad in advance, here's a quick and easy trick. Mix your dressing in the bottom of your salad bowl. Cross the salad spoon and fork over the dressing and gently pile the salad greens above. When you are ready to serve, toss the greens with the dressing — your delicious salad is ready in minutes!

For variety in your tossed salad, try using *leftover meat, poultry,* or *vegetables.* Leftover meat and poultry can be cut into julienne strips or bite-sized pieces and mixed with the vegetables. Leftover vegetables should be dipped in hot water to remove any butter or seasonings that might affect the flavor of your salad. Many homemakers like to marinate leftover vegetables and serve them with the salad or as garnish. If you are going to marinate vegetables, do it while they are hot — the marinade will penetrate farther.

Fruit salads are also popular fare. Fruit for salads should be cut with a stainless steel knife to prevent discoloration. Those fruits that darken after being cut — apples, bananas, pears, etc. — should be placed in fruit juice or salad dressing as soon as they are cut. And for a particularly sparkling flavor treat, the juice you use to protect the fruit may be added to the salad dressing.

Grapefruit and other juicy fruits should be added after the salad is tossed with its dressing. After mixing the greens and other less juicy fruits with the dressing, arrange the grapefruit over the top of the salad. Added in this manner, the fruit will retain its shape, and the juices will not dilute the dressing.

Many salads are particularly nice served in *lettuce cups.* These eye-catching cups are easy to make. Cut the stem end from a head of lettuce and remove. Let the water run into the stem end for several seconds. Separate the leaves, and wash and drain them. Place the small leaves inside the larger ones and gently press the entire mass into a ball. Roll it tightly in a dish towel and chill thoroughly. The result will be crisply attractive lettuce cups ready to hold your favorite salad.

Tossed salads should be prepared in a deep bowl — deep enough to permit you to toss the salad greens without spilling them. For a salad you want to show off, you may transfer the tossed ingredients to a low, broad salad bowl or a deep platter. For years, the traditional salad bowls have been wooden ones. You can clean these by wiping them with a paper cloth. But periodically they require scrubbing and setting in the sun to dry. For today's time-conscious homemakers, there are a wide variety of colors and styles available in easy-to-clean ceramic, glass, and plastic salad bowls.

When you are planning your salad, follow the principles of color and texture contrast. Be sure your salad harmonizes with the other course — but adds a color accent as well. The classic example of a tomato aspic served with a rare roast beef illustrates what is meant by lack of color accent! But that same tomato aspic would be just what is needed with a chicken pie, a casserole, or any main dish which lacked bright color. Similarly, green salads introduce color notes to your dinner table.

Be aware of texture contrast, too. Smooth main dishes — like a la king dishes; meat, gravy, and mashed potatoes; or a meat pie — need the crisp, crunchy texture of a fresh garden salad. You'll find that salads can contrast nicely with one another, too. When you serve potato salad with the main course, try adding a cole slaw with tangy dressing — it will highlight your entire meal.

Dried Beef and Fresh Vegetable Salad (page 14)

special salad entrees

For a marvelously easy-to-prepare meal, few entrees surpass a salad. Served on luncheon or dinner plates with bread, butter, a beverage, and perhaps a special dessert, these salad entrees are unexcelled for ease of preparation, nutrition, and eye-appeal.

Southern homemakers enjoy making entree salads for their families and friends. They mix meats . . . fish . . . chicken . . . vegetable-and-fruit combinations . . . fruit-and-cheese combinations . . . vegetable-and-cheese combinations into hearty, vitamin-filled, appetite-arousing main dish salads.

Think how your family and guests will enjoy sitting down to Glory Salad with an Unusual Honey Dressing. And imagine how beautiful Melon Boat Salad will look on your table! For a touch of Rome, serve Otavio Veal Salad at your next luncheon. Before you know it, you'll have earned an enviable reputation as a maker of magnificent entree salads!

That reputation is yours to have with the recipes you'll find in the pages that follow. Page after page tells you how to prepare elegant, filling, special salad entrees you'll be proud to serve at every meal. And don't forget the wonderful bonus waiting for you when you feature salad entrees — few calories and much eating pleasure!

11

HONEY BOWL

1 lge. can whole apricots	1/2 c. brandy
1 lge. can peach halves	1 c. dark honey
1 lge. can pineapple slices	2 sticks cinnamon
1 bottle red cherries	Slivered peel of 1 orange

Drain the fruits and reserve 2 cups of the juice. Arrange the fruits in a glass bowl, placing the pineapple in the center and the cherries on top. Pour the brandy over the top. Combine the honey, reserved juice, cinnamon and orange peel in a saucepan and simmer for 30 minutes or until peel is tender. Cool, then pour over the fruits. Chill for several hours before serving.

Mrs. Frank Gheen, Jr., San Antonio, Texas

MELON BOAT SALAD

1 c. pineapple chunks	1 honeydew melon, quartered
1 c. fresh strawberries	1 tbsp. honey
1 c. orange sections	1/2 c. French dressing

Combine the pineapple, strawberries and orange sections and spoon into melon quarters. Add the honey to the French dressing and shake to mix well. Serve with the melon boats.

Mrs. Freddie Gussler, Cherokee, Kentucky

SUMMER SUNSET SALAD

1 sm. head lettuce	1/3 c. salad oil
1 c. cottage cheese	3 tsp. lemon juice
1 c. blueberries	1/2 tsp. salt
2 oranges, peeled and sliced	1/3 c. liquid honey

Arrange the lettuce leaves on salad plates. Mound the cottage cheese in the center of each salad plate and surround with a circle of blueberries. Arrange the half slices of oranges around the edge. Combine the salad oil, lemon juice and salt and add the honey slowly, beating constantly. Chill in a tightly covered jar and mix well before serving with the salad. 4 servings.

Paulette Cosby, Stratford, Oklahoma

GLORY SALAD WITH HONEY DRESSING

1 tbsp. sugar	3 med. bananas
1/8 tsp. cinnamon	1 med. peeled avocado, sliced
Dash of nutmeg	3/4 c. grapes, halved and
1 3-oz. package cream cheese	seeded
1 lge. grapefruit	3 c. shredded lettuce

Combine the sugar, cinnamon and nutmeg. Shape the cream cheese into 8 balls and roll in the sugar mixture. Section the grapefruit over a bowl and reserve 3 tablespoons grapefruit juice. Flute the bananas with fork tines and cut into 1/4-inch slices. Sprinkle the bananas and avocado with reserved grapefruit juice. Arrange the bananas, avocado, grapefruit and grapes on a bed of shredded lettuce. Garnish with the cheese balls.

Honey Dressing

1/4 c. salad oil	1/2 tsp. salt
3 tbsp. honey	Dash of pepper
1/4 c. vinegar	1/4 c. water

Combine all of the ingredients and shake well. Serve with the salad.

Genevieve Miller, St. Petersburg, Florida

HOT-SAUCED FRUIT SALAD

1 lge. pineapple	2 tbsp. frozen orange juice
3 or 4 oranges, sectioned	concentrate, thawed
1 sm. grapefruit, sectioned	1/2 tsp. sugar
Strawberry halves or raspberries	1/4 tsp. hot sauce
1 or 2 bananas, sliced	1 tbsp. lemon juice
Melon balls (opt.)	1/2 c. mayonnaise
3/4 tsp. salt	1/2 c. sour cream

Halve the pineapple lengthwise through the green top. Scoop out fruit and cut into cubes. Prepare the oranges, grapefruit, strawberry halves, bananas and melon balls or other fruit in season to make about 1 1/2 quarts fruit. Blend the salt, undiluted orange juice concentrate, sugar, hot sauce and lemon juice into mayonnaise, then stir in the sour cream. Arrange fruit in pineapple halves and serve with sour cream dressing. 6-8 servings.

Hot-Sauced Fruit Salad (above)

DRIED BEEF AND FRESH VEGETABLE SALAD

Leaf lettuce	Swiss cheese strips
Dried beef	Fresh tomato wedges
Fresh cucumber slices	Watercress
Hard-cooked egg slices	Oil and vinegar dressing
Fresh radish slices	

Place the lettuce in a salad bowl to cover bottom and side. Arrange the dried beef, cucumber slices, egg slices, radish slices, cheese strips and tomato wedges in desired pattern on the lettuce. Garnish with watercress and serve with the dressing.

Photograph for this recipe on page 10.

CHEF'S SPECIAL SALAD BOWL

1 head romaine	1 c. chili sauce
1 bunch chicory	1 tbsp. grated onion
1 bunch escarole	1/2 dill pickle, diced
1/2 c. thin ham strips	1 clove of garlic, mashed
1 c. roast beef cubes	1 tbsp. chopped parsley
1 c. Swiss cheese strips	1/2 tsp. salt
1 c. olive oil	1/2 tsp. sugar
1 c. wine vinegar	Pepper to taste
1 c. catsup	

Tear the greens into bite-sized pieces and add the ham, roast beef and cheese. Combine the remaining ingredients for the dressing and mix well. Add enough of the dressing to the greens to coat well, then toss. Garnish with peeled and quartered tomatoes and hard-boiled egg halves.

Mrs. W. A. Giberson, Brunswick, Georgia

EMPEROR SALAD

2 tsp. minced onion	2 hard-cooked eggs, chopped
2 tsp. vinegar	1 cucumber, chopped
1/2 c. mayonnaise	1 green pepper, chopped
3/8 c. milk or cream	1 carrot, chopped
6 slivered slices tongue	2 tomatoes, chopped
1/4 lb. slivered Swiss cheese	

Combine the onion, vinegar, mayonnaise and milk and mix well. Combine the remaining ingredients in a salad bowl and toss with the dressing. 6 servings.

Mrs. C. R. Webster, Jackson, Mississippi

MOBILE HAM SALAD

1/2 c. cubed cooked ham	2 hard-cooked eggs, chopped
1/2 c. diced Swiss cheese	1 c. diced celery

Salt and pepper to taste
2 tbsp. chopped sweet pickle
2 tbsp. minced green onion
   and tops

2 tbsp. chopped pimento
1/2 c. mayonnaise
2 c. shredded lettuce

Combine all the ingredients except lettuce and toss lightly. Refrigerate until ready to serve. Add the lettuce and toss lightly to combine. Garnish with slices of tomato if desired. 6 servings.

Ruth Gurr, Mobile, Alabama

AVOCADO SUPER SALAD

1 head lettuce
Curly endive
1 8 3/4-oz. can kidney beans
1/2 med. cucumber, sliced
1/2 c. sliced sharp cheese
1 1/2 c. sliced cooked ham
2 hard-cooked eggs, sliced
2 sweet pickles, sliced
1/2 bell pepper, diced

3 green onions, chopped
1/2 c. diagonally cut celery
10 cherry tomatoes, halved
1 lge. California avocado,
   sliced
3/4 c. salad dressing
1/2 c. catsup
1 tbsp. chopped parsley

Place the lettuce and endive on a platter. Rinse and drain the kidney beans. Arrange the kidney beans, cucumber, cheese, ham, eggs, pickles, bell pepper, onions, celery, tomatoes and avocado on lettuce mixture. Mix remaining ingredients and serve with the salad.

Avocado Super Salad (above)

15

OTAVIO VEAL SALAD

1 c. veal broth
2 cubes beef bouillon
2 env. unflavored gelatin
2 tbsp. lemon juice
1 c. mayonnaise
1 c. diced celery

1 c. green grapes
2 lb. cooked cubed veal
Salt to taste
1/2 c. toasted slivered
  almonds

Heat the veal broth and add the bouillon. Stir until the bouillon is dissolved. Soften the gelatin in 1/2 cup water and dissolve in the bouillon mixture. Chill until thickened. Fold in all of the ingredients except the almonds and mix well. Place in a 1 1/2-quart mold and chill until firm. Sprinkle the salad with almonds. May be garnished with chilled cranberry sauce, sliced avocado strips, salad fruits and pineapple chunks. 8 servings.

Jessie Mae Jacobs, Apoka, Florida

STUFFED ARTICHOKE SALAD

1 6-oz. can water chestnuts
2 c. cooked cubed chicken
1/4 c. finely diced celery

3/4 c. mayonnaise
4 artichokes
1 tbsp. salt

Fresh Vegetable Salad (page 17)

16

2 tbsp. salad oil	12 stuffed olives
1/2 lemon, cut up	1 tbsp. capers
1 clove of garlic	

Drain the water chestnuts and cut into strips. Combine with the chicken, celery and mayonnaise, tossing lightly with a fork. Refrigerate for several hours. Cut the stems from the artichokes and place in boiling water to cover. Add the salt, oil, lemon and garlic and cook for about 1 hour. Drain and cool, then refrigerate for several hours. Spread the leafy spines of the cooled artichokes carefully from the tip so the inner leaves can be removed. Use a spoon to remove the heart. Fill the cavity with chilled chicken salad. Garnish with the olives and sprinkle with the capers. 4 servings.

Margaret Lopp, Chandler, Arizona

GENTLEMAN'S SALAD

2 hard-boiled eggs, halved	3 lge. tomatoes, sliced
1 sm. can deviled ham	1 green bell pepper, sliced
1 lge. avocado, diced	2 oz. Roquefort cheese,
1 c. diced celery	crumbled
1 chopped pimento	8 slices fried bacon,
Homemade mayonnaise	crumbled
1 head of iceberg lettuce	Chopped chives to taste

Remove the yolks from egg halves and mash. Add the deviled ham and mix well. Fill the egg halves with the ham mixture and then cut in half. Combine the avocado, celery and pimento and mix gently. Add a small amount of mayonnaise and mix gently until moistened. Place in the center of a bowl. Cut the lettuce into wedges and arrange with the tomatoes, and pepper around the avocado mixture. Top with the crumbled cheese, bacon, chives and stuffed eggs. 4 servings.

Byron Avant, West Palm Beach, Florida

FRESH VEGETABLE SALAD

Fresh asparagus	Sliced cucumbers
Italian salad dressing	Fresh mushrooms
Fresh chick-peas	Cauliflowerets
Chopped hard-boiled eggs	Salad tomatoes
Pimento-stuffed green olives	Lettuce
Ripe olives	

Wash the asparagus and break off stalk as far down as snaps easily. Remove scales with a knife and wash again to remove sand. Place in a saucepan and add 1 inch boiling, salted water. Bring to boiling point and cook for 5 minutes. Reduce heat and cover. Cook for 15 minutes or until asparagus is crisp-tender, then drain. Cover with Italian salad dressing and chill overnight. Cook the chick-peas in boiling, salted water until crisp-tender, then drain. Chill. Drain the asparagus and reserve salad dressing. Arrange the asparagus, eggs, green olives, ripe olives, cucumbers, mushrooms, cauliflowerets, tomatoes and chick-peas on a lettuce-lined platter. Garnish center with luncheon meat and serve with reserved dressing.

Raisin Mosaic Salad Ball (below)

RAISIN MOSAIC SALAD BALL

1 c. dark seedless raisins	1 tsp. lemon juice
1/4 c. sherry	1 firm head western iceberg
1 c. diced cantaloupe	lettuce
1 c. diced fresh pears	Cream Cheese Garnish
1 c. chopped or sliced celery	Cantaloupe crescents
1 8-oz. package cream cheese	Sliced ham rolls
1/2 tsp. salt	White asparagus spears
3 drops of hot sauce	Cherry tomatoes
2 tsp. grated onion	Ripe olives

Combine the raisins with sherry in a bowl and let stand for several hours or overnight, stirring several times. Chill the diced cantaloupe, pears and celery. Drain the raisins, reserving 2 tablespoons for garnish. Toss remaining raisins with diced cantaloupe, pears and celery. Beat the cream cheese until smooth and fluffy, then beat in the salt, hot sauce, onion and lemon juice. Drain the pear mixture and add to cream cheese mixture. Mix lightly but well. Cut the lettuce into 4 thick slices. Shape the pear mixture into 4 balls and place 1 on top of each lettuce slice. Press Cream Cheese Garnish through a pastry tube around bottom of fruit ball and over top. Garnish with reserved raisins, cantaloupe crescents, ham rolls, asparagus spears, cherry tomatoes and ripe olives. 4 servings.

Cream Cheese Garnish

1 3-oz. package plain or	1 tbsp. mayonnaise
pimento cream cheese	

Beat the cream cheese and mayonnaise in a bowl until smooth.

STUFFED TOMATOES IN ASPIC

3/4 c. diced celery	1/8 tsp. celery salt
1 1/4 c. chopped chicken	6 sm. tomatoes
1/3 c. mayonnaise	1 3-cup recipe tomato aspic
1/2 tsp. salt	1 green pepper, sliced
1/8 tsp. pepper	Stuffed olives, sliced

Combine the celery, chicken, mayonnaise, salt, pepper and celery salt and mix well. Cut the tops from the tomatoes and scoop out the pulp. Fill the tomatoes with the chicken mixture and then chill. Cover the bottom of individual molds with the aspic and place the green pepper and olives in bottom of mold. Chill until set. Place tomatoes, upside down in molds and add aspic to cover. Chill until set. Unmold on lettuce leaves and serve with a sharp salad dressing. 6 servings.

Mrs. R. B. Jones, Louisville, Kentucky

DEVILED EGGS IN TOMATO ASPIC

6 hard-cooked eggs	Dash of pepper
1/4 c. mayonnaise	2 tbsp. chopped stuffed olives
2 tsp. prepared mustard	1 3-oz. package seasoned
2 tbsp. minced onion	tomato gelatin
1/4 tsp. salt	

Cut the eggs into halves lengthwise and remove and mash the yolks. Blend the yolks with mayonnaise, mustard, onion, salt, pepper and olives. Stuff the yolk mixture into egg whites and place the halves together. Chill. Prepare the gelatin according to package directions, then pour 1/2 cup into a 1-quart ring mold. Chill until partially set. Arrange the eggs in mold and pour the remaining gelatin over eggs. Chill until firm. Unmold onto salad platter and garnish as desired. 4-6 servings.

Mrs. Wilbur Williams, Baton Rouge, Louisiana

LOBSTER SALAD WITH TOMATO ASPIC RING

2 tbsp. unflavored gelatin	1 c. chopped cooked lobster
4 c. tomato juice	1/4 c. French dressing
2 c. chopped celery	2 hard-cooked eggs, chopped
2 tbsp. lemon juice	Mayonnaise to taste

Soften the gelatin in 1/2 cup of the tomato juice. Heat the remaining tomato juice and add the gelatin mixture, then stir until the gelatin is dissolved. Chill until slightly thickened, then add 1 cup celery and the lemon juice. Pour into an oiled 4 1/2 to 5-cup ring mold and chill until firm. Marinate the lobster in the French dressing for 1 hour and then drain. Add the remaining celery, eggs and enough mayonnaise to moisten. Toss until well blended. Unmold the aspic ring onto lettuce leaves and fill the center with the lobster mixture. 4 servings.

Mrs. W. R. Massey, Tulsa, Oklahoma

Dungeness Crab Salad (below)

DUNGENESS CRAB SALAD

1 lb. fresh or frozen
  dungeness crab meat
1   14 or 15-oz. can artichoke
  hearts
1   8-oz. can cut green beans
2 hard-cooked eggs, chopped
1/2 c. sliced celery
1/4 c. sliced fresh cauliflower
1/4 c. sliced cucumber

1/4 c. sliced green pepper
1 tsp. salt
1/4 tsp. pepper
3/4 c. Thousand Island
  dressing
6 tomato slices
6 lettuce leaves
Radish slices

Thaw the frozen crab meat. Drain the crab meat and remove any shell or cartilage. Cut the crab meat into 1/2-inch pieces. Drain the artichoke hearts and cut
into fourths. Drain the beans. Combine all ingredients except the tomato slices,
lettuce and radish slices in a bowl and toss lightly. Arrange a tomato slice on
each lettuce leaf. Place about 1 cup crab mixture on each tomato slice and
garnish with radish slices. Three 6 1/2 or 7 1/2-ounce cans crab meat, drained,
may be substituted for fresh crab meat. 6 servings.

CALIFORNIA CRAB SALAD

1 clove of garlic, minced
1 tsp. salt
2 tbsp. capers
2 tbsp. chopped canned green
  chilies
2 tbsp. chopped pimento
2 tbsp. wine vinegar with
  tarragon
1/2 c. olive or salad oil
Freshly ground pepper to taste

Dash of hot sauce
8-oz. canned or frozen cooked
  crab
1 lge. avocado, quartered and
  sliced
1 med. red onion, sliced
2 tomatoes, sliced into thin
  wedges
1 1/2 to 2 qt. salad greens

Combine the garlic, salt, capers, chilies, pimento, vinegar, oil, pepper and hot sauce in a jar and shake until well blended. Place the remaining ingredients in a large salad bowl and toss with the dressing. 3-4 servings.

Mrs. Thomas A. Bell, Gallup, New Mexico

GREEN GODDESS SHRIMP SALAD

1/2 head romaine	1/4 tsp. garlic juice
1 stalk chicory	1/2 tsp. salt
1 head lettuce	1 tsp. Worcestershire sauce
3 med. tomatoes	2 tbsp. anchovy paste
2 c. small cooked shrimp	1 c. mayonnaise
1/2 c. drained julienne beets	3 tbsp. chopped chives

Tear the romaine, chicory and lettuce into bite-sized pieces and arrange on salad plates. Peel the tomatoes and cut into quarters, then arrange on the greens. Top with the shrimp and beets. Combine the remaining ingredients for the dressing and mix well. Serve with the salad.

Mrs. R. B. Nevil, McKinney, Texas

SHRIMP PARADISE SALAD

1 pineapple	2 oranges
1 avocado	3/4 lb. cooked peeled shrimp
1 tbsp. orange juice	

Cut the pineapple in half lengthwise and remove the core. Cut the pulp from the pineapple, leaving 1/2-inch shells. Cut the pulp into small chunks. Cut the avocado in half lengthwise and remove the seed. Peel and slice, then sprinkle with the orange juice. Peel and dice the oranges. Combine the pineapple chunks, avocado and oranges and fill the pineapple shells. Top with the shrimp and serve cold. 6 servings.

Carolyn Bassett, Jacksonville, Florida

SALMON CAESAR

1 clove of garlic	1/4 c. lemon juice
2/3 c. oil	2 eggs, beaten
2 qt. torn romaine	1/2 c. grated Parmesan cheese
1/2 tsp. salt	1 1/2 c. croutons
Freshly ground pepper	1 1-lb. can salmon, flaked
1 onion, thinly sliced	

Combine the garlic and the oil and let stand at room temperature for 3 hours. Remove the garlic. Place the romaine in a large salad bowl and add the salt, pepper, onion and oil. Toss well. Add the lemon juice to the eggs, beating constantly. Pour over the romaine mixture and toss well. Sprinkle with the cheese and add the croutons and salmon. Toss until just mixed and serve immediately.

Mrs. Lawrence Graham, Portsmouth, Virginia

hearty meat salads

Take bite-sized pieces of beef, pork, ham, veal, or specialty meats . . . mix them with two or three salad greens . . . add croutons, bits of onion, or chunks of green pepper for flavor and texture contrast . . . sprinkle with your favorite dressing . . . toss well — then serve your hungry family one of the most flavorful and nutritious dishes they could have: a hearty meat salad!

Homemakers from Maryland to Texas serve these rib-sticking salads to their families and guests on every possible occasion. They know that meat salads are the perfect main dish as well as attractive appetizers. They know, too, that meat salads, for all their appetite-arousing appearance, are low in both cost and calories and high in needed vitamin and mineral values.

Many of the salad recipes you'll find in the following pages can be prepared with leftovers from a roast. And while getting the most for your meat dollar, you'll also be serving your family unforgettably flavorful salads. Transform that leftover corned beef into French Beef Salad. Bring a touch of old New Orleans to your table by serving veal in a Jean Lafitte Salad — an old southern meat favorite dressed up in new fashion.

These are just two of the recipes you'll discover in the pages that follow. You're certain to find at least one you'll want to try — today!

23

Meat, poultry, and seafood salads are hearty enough for main dishes — or just right as appetizer salads with a light main course. If you are serving these salads as the entree, allow about one cup per serving. Plan on half that portion for appetizer salads.

These versatile salads are great budget aids. You can prepare a flavorful meat, poultry, or seafood salad with leftovers from your roast or dinner of the night before. If you are short on meat, try adding some leftover vegetables or julienne strips of cheese. The result will probably be a brand-new flavor treat for your appreciative family.

The main ingredients of meat, poultry, and seafood salads tend to be smooth in texture and heavy in flavor. Provide texture and flavor contrast by including one or two tablespoons of chopped green peppers, cucumber, celery,

general directions
FOR MEAT, POULTRY, & SEAFOOD SALADS

water chestnuts, or pickles. These crisp and crunchy tidbits will do much to lift the taste of your salad to new heights.

Meats suitable for salads include ham, roast beef, corned beef, veal, lamb, or any of the many luncheon meats. The recipe may call for you to julienne the meat — cut it into long, thin strips. This method is often used to prepare chef or Caesar salads. Other methods used to prepare meat for salads include cubing (cutting into 3/4- to one-inch squares), dicing (cutting into smaller cubes — about 1/4- to 1/2-inch pieces), chopping (cutting into pieces about the size of peas), or mincing (cutting into even smaller pieces).

Poultry salads — especially chicken — are among the most popular of all salads. To prepare chicken for salad, place a five- to six-pound stewing chicken (or two broiler-fryers) in a cooking pot. These quantities yield about five cups of chicken. Cover it with two quarts of water. In a cheesecloth bag place two parsley sprigs, four chopped celery stalks, a chopped carrot, and a small onion. Put the bag into the cooking pot and add salt and pepper to taste. Cook the chicken for about two and a half hours. This subtle blend of flavors will give your chicken a flavor lift.

Seafood salads are particularly popular in the Southland where the bounty from seas and rivers is abundant. These salads offer creative homemakers many opportunities for flavor and color contrast — as in a crab or shrimp salad served in crisp lettuce cups.

One other bonus meat, poultry, and seafood salads bring to homemakers is low calories. The chart on the opposite page gives calorie values for the main ingredients most often used in preparing these salads:

MEAT, POULTRY, AND SEAFOOD CALORIE CHART

FOOD	AMOUNT	CALORIES
BACON, Canadian	1 ounce	65
BACON, med. fat, broiled or fried	2 slices	95
BEEF, cooked:		
chuck	3 ounces	245
round	3 ounces	220
rump	3 ounces	320
steak	3 ounces	330
BEEF, corned	3 ounces	180
CHICKEN:		
broilers	8 ounces	370
canned, boned	3 ounces	170
creamed	1/2 cup	160
hens, stewing chickens	4 ounces	340
roasters	4 ounces	225
CLAMS:		
canned, solids and liquid	3 ounces	45
raw	4 ounces	90
COD:		
dried	1 ounce	105
raw	4 ounces	85
CRABS, Atlantic and Pacific		
hard-shell	3 ounces	90
FLOUNDER	4 ounces	80
FRANKFURTER	one	155
HADDOCK, broiled:		
1 steak	4'' x 3'' x ½''	228
1 pound		825
HERRING, smoked, kippered	3 ounces	180
LAMB:		
leg roast	3 ounces	235
shoulder roast	3 ounces	285
LIVERWURST	2 ounces	175
LOBSTER	3 ounces	80
MACKEREL, canned	3 ounces	155
OYSTERS, raw	1 cup (13-19 medium size)	160
PERCH FILLET	3 ounces	195
PORK:		
ham, boiled	2 ounces	170
ham, fresh cooked	3 ounces	340
ham, smoke cooked	3 ounces	290
loin	3 ounces	285
SALMON:		
broiled or baked	4'' x 3'' x ½''	205
canned, pink	3 ounces	120
canned, red	3 ounces	145
SARDINES, oil-pack, drained	3 ounces	180
SAUSAGE:		
pork	4 ounces	340
Vienna	2 ounces	135
SCALLOPS	4 ounces	90
SHAD, raw	3 ounces	170
SHRIMP, canned or raw	3 ounces	110
SWORDFISH, broiled	3 ounces	150
TONGUE, beef	3 ounces	205
TUNA, canned, drained	3 ounces	170
TURKEY	4 ounces	305
VEAL, shoulder	3 ounces	305

CONGEALED CORNED BEEF SALAD

1 can beef consomme	1 c. chopped celery
1 pkg. lemon gelatin	1 sm. onion, chopped
1 can corned beef, chopped	2 tbsp. chopped pimento (opt.)
1 c. salad dressing or mayonnaise	3 hard-cooked eggs, chopped

Add enough water to the consomme to make 2 cups liquid and pour into a saucepan. Bring to a boil and stir in gelatin until dissolved. Chill until thickened. Fold in the corned beef, salad dressing, celery, onion, pimento and eggs. Pour into mold and chill until firm. 8 servings.

Mrs. Ed Grubbs, Baltimore, Maryland

GOURMET BEEF SALAD

1/3 c. warm water	1/4 c. sliced stuffed green olives
1/2 c. seedless raisins	1/4 c. slivered almonds
2 c. cold 2-in. long roast beef strips	1 tbsp. chopped pimento
1 1/2 c. fresh pineapple pieces	1/4 tsp. salt
1/2 c. chopped celery	1/2 c. sour cream
1/2 sm. green pepper, cut in strips	Grated coconut (opt.)

Mix the water and raisins and soak for 15 minutes. Drain. Combine the roast beef, raisins, pineapple, celery, green pepper, olives, almonds, pimento and salt in a bowl and toss lightly. Add the sour cream and mix until all ingredients are coated. Chill for 2 to 3 hours. Serve topped with coconut. 6 servings.

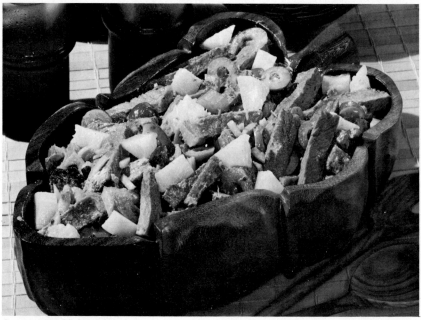

Gourmet Beef Salad (above)

ASPARAGUS-MEAT MOLD

1 env. unflavored gelatin	1 c. asparagus tips
1/4 c. cold water	1/4 c. chopped green pepper
1 1/2 c. hot meat broth	1/2 c. chopped celery
2 c. chopped cooked meat	1/2 tsp. salt

Soften the gelatin in 1/4 cup cold water, then add the hot meat broth and stir until dissolved. Chill until partially set. Arrange the meat, asparagus, pepper and celery in a mold and season with the salt. Add the gelatin and chill until firm. Unmold on a bed of crisp lettuce and garnish with mayonnaise and olives. 6 servings.

Mrs. C. R. Ledbetter, Black Rock, Arkansas

FRENCH BEEF SALAD

1/2 c. French dressing	1/4 c. chopped sweet pickles
2 c. diced cooked beef	2 hard-cooked eggs, diced
1/2 c. coarsely grated carrots	1/2 c. mayonnaise
1/2 c. diced cooked potatoes	4 to 6 lettuce cups
1/2 c. cooked green beans	

Pour the French dressing over the beef and chill for 1 hour or longer. Chill the remaining ingredients. Combine the beef, carrots, potatoes, beans, pickles and eggs. Add the mayonnaise and mix lightly. Serve the salad in lettuce cups. 4-6 servings.

Mrs. Glenn Moore, Tulsa, Oklahoma

CAPRI BEEF SALAD

2 lb. round steak	1 c. chopped green peppers
1 8-oz. bottle Italian dressing	1/2 c. pimento strips
2 c. sliced carrots, cooked	1 c. red onion rings
2 c. cooked lima beans, drained	1 head lettuce

Cut the steak into small strips and brown in a small amount of the Italian dressing. Combine the steak, carrots, beans, green peppers, pimento, onion and remaining dressing, tossing to mix. Refrigerate until well chilled. Tear the lettuce into bite-sized pieces and toss with the steak mixture. 6 servings.

Mrs. H. M. Polk, Abilene, Texas

SALAD DE VACA

1 lb. ground beef	1 tbsp. chili powder
1/4 c. chopped onion	4 c. shredded lettuce
2 c. drained kidney beans	1/2 c. sliced green onions
1/2 c. bottled French dressing	2 c. shredded Cheddar cheese

Brown the ground beef in a skillet, then add the onion and cook until tender. Stir in the beans, French dressing, 1/2 cup water and chili powder and simmer for 15 minutes. Combine the lettuce and green onions and add the meat sauce and 1 1/2 cups cheese. Toss lightly and then sprinkle with the remaining cheese. Serve with crisp tortillas.

Mrs. J. B. Garner, Anderson, South Carolina

BEEFBURGER LOAF

2 env. unflavored gelatin	2 lb. ground beef
2 beef bouillon cubes	1/2 c. finely chopped onions
3/4 c. salad dressing	1/4 c. sliced stuffed olives

Soften the gelatin in 1/2 cup cold water and heat over low heat, stirring until dissolved. Dissolve the bouillon cubes in 1 1/2 cups boiling water and add to the gelatin mixture. Cool. Add the gelatin mixture gradually to the salad dressing, mixing until well blended. Chill until slightly thickened. Brown the ground beef and add onions and cook until tender. Drain and cool. Fold the ground beef mixture and olives into gelatin mixture, then pour into 8 x 4 x 2-inch pan. Chill until firm. Unmold to serve. 8 servings.

Mrs. Edward McVickar, Knoxville, Tennessee

TACO SALAD

1 lb. hamburger	1/2 tsp. hot sauce
1 can solid-pack tomatoes	1/2 15-oz. can refried beans
1 c. shredded cheese	1 6-oz. package corn chips
2 heads lettuce, shredded	Salt and pepper to taste
1/2 c. chopped green onions	

Brown the hamburger in a skillet and drain. Drain the tomatoes and reserve the juice, then cut up the tomatoes. Add the tomatoes, cheese, lettuce and onions to the hamburger. Combine the reserved tomato juice, hot sauce and beans and simmer until heated through. Add to the hamburger mixture and toss well. Add the corn chips, salt and pepper and serve immediately.

Mrs. D. T. Kirkland, Baton Rouge, Louisiana

MAINSTAY SALAD

1 No. 2 can red kidney beans	2 hard-cooked eggs, chopped
2 c. julienne cooked beef or	2 tbsp. sliced sweet pickle
pork	1/4 c. mayonnaise
1 c. chopped celery	1 tbsp. chili sauce
1/4 c. chopped onion	1 tsp. salt

Drain the beans and chill all ingredients. Combine all the ingredients and toss lightly. Chill in a covered bowl for 30 minutes, then serve in lettuce cups. 4-6 servings.

Mrs. Aline Wilson, Ringgold, Louisiana

TENDERLOIN SALAD

1 lb. lean beef tenderloin,	1 lb. lean veal, cooked
cooked	1 c. diced celery

1/4 c. diced olives   Mayonnaise to taste
3/4 lb. brick cheese, diced

Cool the beef and veal, then dice. Combine all the ingredients with just enough mayonnaise to moisten. Serve on lettuce. 12 servings.

Mrs. Russell Blankenship, Huntington, West Virginia

MADRAS MEAT SALAD

1 12-oz. can roast beef	1 c. chopped pecans
1 can sm. lima beans, drained	Chopped onion to taste
4 hard-boiled eggs, chopped	Chopped olives to taste
1 c. chopped celery	Mayonnaise to taste

Cut the roast beef into small pieces and add the remaining ingredients. Mix well and serve at room temperature.

Mrs. Herman Cates, Madras, Georgia

JEAN LAFITTE SALAD

2 c. cooked diced meat	1 c. French dressing
3/4 c. cooked diced potatoes	4 sweet pickles, chopped
3/4 c. cooked diced carrots	2 hard-boiled eggs, chopped
3/4 c. cooked green beans, drained	1 c. mayonnaise

Combine the meat and vegetables and add the French dressing. Mix well and then marinate for 1 hour. Add the pickles, eggs and mayonnaise and mix well. Chill and then serve on lettuce. 8 servings.

Mrs. Earl Moeller, San Antonio, Texas

JELLIED VEAL

2 tbsp. unflavored gelatin	1/2 c. finely diced carrots
2 c. beef consomme	1 c. diced celery
3 c. diced veal or chicken	Tomato slices
1 1/2 tsp. salt	1 sm. can peas, drained

Soften the gelatin in 1/2 cup consomme, then add to the remaining consomme. Heat, stirring, until dissolved. Add the remaining ingredients except the tomatoes and peas. Arrange the tomatoes and peas in bottom of individual dishes and add the gelatin mixture. Chill until firm. Unmold onto lettuce leaf and garnish.

Mrs. N. J. Bell, Louisville, Kentucky

NEW SALEM SAUSAGE SALAD

2 1/2 lb. sausage links	1/4 c. chopped sweet pickle
7 oz. shell macaroni	1/2 c. mayonnaise
1/2 c. shredded Cheddar cheese	1/2 c. sour cream
1/2 c. sliced celery	1 tsp. lemon juice
1/4 c. chopped green pepper	1/2 tsp. onion salt

Fry the sausage in a skillet until done and then drain. Cook the macaroni according to package directions and drain. Cut the sausage into small pieces and add the macaroni, cheese, celery, green pepper and pickle. Blend the remaining ingredients together and add to the sausage mixture. Toss until well combined.

Mrs. A. M. Carpenter, Savannah, Georgia

PARTY PORK CROWN

1 3-oz. package celery gelatin	1 12-oz. can pork luncheon
1 tbsp. cider vinegar	meat
1/2 c. mayonnaise	1 8-oz. can peas, drained
1/2 tsp. prepared mustard	Romaine leaves
1/4 tsp. salt	

Dissolve the gelatin in 1 cup hot water, then add 1/2 cup cold water and vinegar. Beat in the mayonnaise, mustard and salt and pour into a shallow pan. Freeze for 20 minutes, then spoon into a medium bowl and beat until light. Dice the luncheon meat and fold into the gelatin mixture with the peas. Spoon into a 4-cup ring mold and chill until firm. Place the romaine leaves on a serving plate and unmold the salad on the leaves. 4-6 servings.

Mrs. R. H. Fulton, Austin, Texas

PORK CHOP SALAD

1 lb. pork chops	1/2 c. mayonnaise
1 tbsp. salt	1 tbsp. prepared mustard
1 sm. onion, diced	1 hard-boiled egg, diced
1/2 bell pepper, diced	1/2 c. diced olives
1 c. diced celery	1/2 c. diced sweet pickles

Sprinkle the pork chops with the salt and refrigerate for 12 hours. Rinse the chops and place in a pan, adding enough water to cover. Cook until tender. Cool chops, then trim off fat and dice the meat. Mix with the remaining ingredients and serve on lettuce leaves. 6 servings.

Mrs. R. L. Patrick, Engelhard, North Carolina

PORK SALAD

2 env. unflavored gelatin
2 1/2 c. milk
1/4 c. butter
3 tbsp. flour
1 1/2 c. salad dressing
1/2 tsp. salt
1/2 c. diced unpeeled apple
Dash of pepper

Dash of monosodium glutamate
1/2 tsp. grated onion
3 c. diced cooked pork
1 c. thinly sliced celery
1/2 c. sliced stuffed olives
1/2 c. slivered blanched
  almonds
3/4 c. heavy cream, whipped

Soften the gelatin in 1/2 cup cold milk. Melt the butter over low heat and blend in the flour. Add the remaining milk and cook until smooth and creamy, stirring constantly. Add the gelatin mixture, stirring until dissolved, then blend in the salad dressing. Cool. Fold in the remaining ingredients carefully and pour into a ring mold. Refrigerate for at least 2 hours or until set. 6-8 servings.

Mrs. W. G. Grove, New Orleans, Louisiana

PEACHY PORK SALAD

3/4 c. mayonnaise
3/4 tsp. salt
3 c. cubed cooked pork
1 5-oz. can water chestnuts

1 16-oz. can sliced peaches
1 c. green grape halves, seeded
4 c. sliced celery cabbage

Combine the mayonnaise and salt in a bowl. Add the pork and mix lightly. Drain and slice the water chestnuts. Drain the peaches. Add the water chestnuts, peaches, grapes and cabbage to pork mixture and toss lightly. Chill thoroughly. 6-8 servings.

Peachy Pork Salad (above)

Royal Pyramid Salad (below)

ROYAL PYRAMID SALAD

1/2 lb. diced cooked ham or tongue	Shredded lettuce
1/2 c. sliced ripe olives	2 hard-cooked eggs, sliced
2 tbsp. capers	1 1-lb. can asparagus spears,
1/4 c. minced scallions	drained
1 1/2 c. orange pieces	Sliced orange twists
Salad dressing	

Combine the ham, olives, capers, scallions and orange pieces with enough salad dressing to hold ingredients together. Place pyramid-style on lettuce on individual plates. Garnish with egg slices, asparagus spears and orange twists. 4 servings.

DOGES' SALAD

1 head lettuce	5 tbsp. vinegar with garlic
1 lge. onion, chopped	5 tbsp. salad oil
3 stalks celery, chopped	5 tbsp. olive oil
1 tomato, chopped	Lemon juice to taste
1 cucumber, chopped	Pinch of salt
1 hard-cooked egg, chopped	Pepper to taste
1/4 lb. cooked ham, chopped	Oregano to taste
1/4 lb. sharp cheese, grated	8 pitted ripe olives
4 tbsp. grated Parmesan cheese	8 green olives

Tear the lettuce into bite-sized pieces and place in a large salad bowl. Add the onion, celery, tomato, cucumber, egg, ham and cheeses. Combine the vinegar, salad oil, olive oil and lemon juice in a small jar and shake well. Add the salt, pepper and oregano, then pour over the salad. Toss well and top with the olives. 4-8 servings.

Mrs. P. O. Alson, Orlando, Florida

CRUNCHY BAKED HAM SALAD

3 c. cooked diced ham	1 tbsp. lemon juice
1 c. diced celery	1 tbsp. prepared mustard
1/2 c. chopped stuffed green	Dash of pepper
olives	3/4 c. mayonnaise
4 hard-cooked eggs, diced	1 c. crushed potato chips
1/4 c. chopped onion	

Combine all of the ingredients except the potato chips and place in a 8 x 2-inch round baking dish. Sprinkle with the potato chips. Bake at 400 degrees for 20 to 25 minutes.

Kasie Hope, Shelby, North Carolina

DELICIOUS HAM SALAD SANDWICH FILLING

2 c. ground ham	1/4 c. mayonnaise
2 hard-cooked eggs, ground	2 tbsp. horseradish
4 tbsp. ground green pepper	1/4 tsp. onion salt
4 tbsp. ground sweet pickles	Dash of pepper

Combine all of the ingredients and mix well with a fork. Chill for several hours or overnight. 3 cups.

Rebecca Clements, Chatham, Virginia

HAM-KIDNEY BEAN SALAD

1 can kidney beans, drained	1/2 lb. cheese, chopped
1/2 c. chopped celery	1 lb. ham, cut in strips
1/2 c. diced green pepper	2 hard-boiled eggs, sliced
1 onion, cut in rings	Mayonnaise
1/2 c. chopped pickles	

Combine all the ingredients except the mayonnaise and toss. Chill until just before serving. Add enough mayonnaise to moisten and mix carefully. Serve in lettuce cups with hot bread or crackers.

Mrs. Mary Ann Lea, Vilonia, Arkansas

IMPERIAL HAM SALAD

1 1/2 c. diced Smithfield ham	1/3 c. salad dressing
6 hard-cooked eggs, diced	2 tbsp. prepared mustard
1/2 c. diced celery	1 tbsp. lemon juice
1/2 c. sliced gherkins	Salt and pepper

Combine the ham, eggs, celery and gherkins. Blend the salad dressing, mustard and lemon juice together and add to the ham mixture. Toss lightly and season to taste. Garnish with additional salad dressing or mayonnaise and sprinkle with paprika. Serve on lettuce. 6 servings.

Mrs. Donald Warder, Wallingford, Kentucky

HAM MOUSSE

2 c. chopped boiled ham	1 c. heavy cream
2 tsp. prepared mustard	4 tbsp. mayonnaise
1 tsp. horseradish	2 tbsp. unflavored gelatin

Force the ham through a meat chopper twice, then mix with the mustard and horseradish. Whip the cream until stiff and add to the mayonnaise. Soften the gelatin in 1/2 cup cold water and dissolve over hot water. Cool for several minutes, then strain into the cream. Refrigerate for 15 minutes. Fold in the ham mixture. Mix thoroughly and pour into a cold mold. Refrigerate for several hours or until set. Turn out on a serving dish and garnish with lettuce and radish roses. 6 servings.

Mrs. H. L. Cockrum, Houston, Texas

HOT HAM SALAD

4 c. cooked cubed ham	1/2 c. sour cream
1 c. finely chopped ripe olives	Salt and pepper to taste
3 hard-cooked eggs, chopped	Italian herb seasonings
1/2 c. finely chopped celery	to taste
1/4 c. finely chopped onion	1/2 c. grated sharp Cheddar
1/2 c. chopped almonds (opt.)	cheese
1/2 c. mayonnaise	1/2 c. crushed corn chips

Preheat oven to 350 degrees. Combine all the ingredients except the cheese and corn chips. Place in a greased loaf pan and sprinkle with the cheese and chips. Bake for 30 minutes. 10 servings.

Mrs. K. H. Wilson, Meridian, Mississippi

LADY MARGARET'S LUNCHEON SALAD

6 c. shredded lettuce	3/4 c. salad oil
4 ripe tomatoes, chopped	1/3 c. vinegar
3 lge. green peppers, slivered	1 tsp. salt
1 lge. onion, thinly sliced	1 tsp. pepper
1 c. diced cheese	1 tsp. sugar
1 c. diced celery	1 tsp. catsup
6 radishes, thinly sliced	1 tsp. onion powder
1 c. diced cucumbers	1/2 tsp. garlic powder
1 c. cooked diced ham or chicken	

Combine the lettuce, tomatoes, green peppers, onion, cheese, celery, radishes, cucumbers and ham, then toss lightly. Combine the remaining ingredients in a jar and shake well. Pour over the salad and toss. Garnish with ripe olives and serve with hot biscuits or crackers. 8 servings.

Mrs. F. H. Frazier, Louisville, Kentucky

BOLOGNA-DILL SALAD

2 pkg. lemon gelatin	1/2 c. chopped bologna
4 c. creamed cottage cheese	3/4 c. chopped dill pickles

Dissolve the gelatin in 2 cups hot water and stir until dissolved. Add the cheese, bologna and pickles. Chill until slightly thickened, then turn into an 8-inch springform pan. Chill until firm and unmold on lettuce. Garnish with dill pickle slices and radish slices. 4-6 servings.

Mrs. Dean Collins, Parrottsville, Tennessee

SALAD BOLOGNESE

2 env. unflavored gelatin	2 c. diced bologna
1/2 tsp. salt	2 c. grated American cheese
1/2 c. vinegar	1/2 c. diced celery
1/2 c. diced sweet pickles	

Soften the gelatin in 1 cup cold water in a saucepan. Simmer, stirring constantly, until gelatin dissolves. Remove from heat and add 1 1/2 cups water, salt and vinegar. Chill until the mixture is of consistency of unbeaten egg whites. Fold in the remaining ingredients and pour into a 6-cup mold. Chill until firm. Unmold on watercress and serve with mayonnaise thinned with sour cream. Garnish mold with tomato slices, green pepper rings and minced onion.

Mrs. Boyd Call, Heddenite, North Carolina

HOT POTATO-FRANK SALAD

6 strips bacon, chopped	1 1/2 tsp. salt
1 tbsp. flour	1/2 tsp. pepper
1/2 c. chopped green onions with tops	1 tbsp. sugar
	1 lb. wieners, sliced
1/4 c. vinegar	1 qt. hot sliced cooked potatoes

Fry the bacon until crisp and blend in the flour until smooth. Add the onions, vinegar, seasonings, 1/2 cup water and wieners and cook for 5 minutes. Pour over the hot potatoes and mix lightly. 6 servings.

Mrs. George L. Walker, Haines City, Florida

HAWAIIAN SALAD

1 12-oz. can luncheon meat	2 c. coarsely diced celery
1 tbsp. vinegar	1/4 c. chopped green pepper
1 tsp. horseradish	1 c. shredded lettuce
1 c. mayonnaise	2 c. cubed pineapple
2 c. shredded cabbage	

Cut the meat into thin strips and add the vinegar. Combine the remaining ingredients and toss lightly with the meat mixture.

Mrs. Lydia Roddy, Pyote, Texas

ANTIPASTO SALAD

1 1-lb. package lge. shell
    macaroni
1/4 c. diced green onion
1/2 c. diced green pepper
1 c. diced celery
1 c. cherry tomato halves
1 c. whole pitted ripe olives
1 tsp. salt

1/4 tsp. pepper
1 6-oz. package sliced
    processed Swiss cheese
1 4-oz. package sliced Genoa
    salami
Italian-style salad dressing
12 slices hard salami

Cook the macaroni according to package directions, then drain. Combine the onion, green pepper, celery, tomato halves, olives, salt and pepper in a large salad bowl. Add the macaroni and toss lightly. Cut the cheese and Genoa salami into thin strips and add to the macaroni mixture. Add desired amount of salad dressing and toss lightly. Fold each slice of hard salami in half, then into quarters. Place each slice around the rim of the salad bowl. 6 servings.

Photograph for this recipe on page 22.

MEAT-POTATO SALAD

8 to 10 med. cooked potatoes,
    diced
3 hard-cooked eggs, diced
1/2 c. diced cheese
1/4 c. diced onions
3 tbsp. diced green pepper

1/4 c. diced pickles
1 tbsp. celery seed
1 can luncheon meat, diced
1/2 to 3/4 c. salad dressing
Salt and pepper to taste

Combine all of the ingredients and mix well. Garnish with paprika and serve on lettuce. 10-12 servings.

Mrs. Tommy Long, Scottsville, Kentucky

LIVER SALAD

1 lb. calves liver
1 1/2 c. water
1/2 tsp. salt
3 c. grated cabbage
1 tbsp. grated onion (opt.)
3/4 c. salad dressing
1/8 tsp. pepper

1 tsp. celery seed
1 tsp. caraway seed
2 tbsp. vinegar
1 tbsp. sugar
2 tbsp. catsup
1 tsp. Worcestershire sauce

Place the liver in 1 1/2 cups boiling, salted water and cook for 10 minutes, then drain. Grind the liver in a food chopper and add the salt, cabbage and onion. Combine the remaining ingredients and add to the liver mixture. Chill until serving time. 6 servings.

Mrs. L. J. Wallace, Riverdale, Maryland

TROPICAL LAMB SALAD

2 bananas, sliced
2 tbsp. lemon juice
3/4 c. sliced celery
2 c. cooked diced lamb
1 1/2 tsp. prepared mustard

1/4 c. mayonnaise
1/4 c. whole stuffed olives
1/4 c. salted almonds
1/2 tsp. salt

Toss the bananas with the lemon juice and add the celery and lamb. Combine the mustard and mayonnaise and pour over the lamb mixture. Add the olives, almonds and salt, then toss. Refrigerate for 30 minutes, then serve on Boston lettuce and watercress. 4 servings.

Mrs. M. S. Nichok, Murfreesboro, Tennessee

KNACKWURST AND KRAUT SALAD

1 lb. knackwurst
1 16-oz. can sauerkraut
2 tbsp. chopped onion
1/2 c. chopped celery

1/4 c. chopped green pepper
1/2 c. vinegar
1/4 c. salad oil
1/2 c. sugar

Cut the knackwurst in bite-sized pieces. Drain and chop the sauerkraut. Combine the knackwurst, sauerkraut, onion, celery and green pepper in a bowl and chill. Mix the vinegar, oil and sugar. Pour the dressing over salad mixture just before serving and toss lightly. 4 servings.

Knackwurst and Kraut Salad (above)

Curried Pineapple-Turkey Salad (page 51)

poultry salads

For unusual appetizer salads before light meals . . . for entrees at luncheons or parties . . . for buffet salads . . . on every occasion which demands a smoothly textured, flavorful salad, southern homemakers turn to poultry. This long-time favorite of women throughout the Southland makes perfect salads every time, salads such as those you'll find recipes for in this section.

Some of these salads are congealed — like the Chicken Buffet Molds that present elegant chicken salad in a buffet-perfect form. Some mix chicken with complementary fruits — colorful Avocado-Chicken Salad with Almonds is one. Some feature favorite combinations in new dress — try Layered Chicken-Cranberry Party Salad the next time you want to sparkle up a dinner table. And some bring new flavor excitement to chicken — Curried Chicken Salad, for example.

These and the other recipes awaiting you in the pages that follow are home-tested, family-approved favorites created by southern homemakers — women long famous for their ability to bring zest and excitement to every meal.

As you explore this section, you'll find yourself imagining these sure-to-please salads brightening up your table and your menu. Try one tonight — you'll be amazed at the way it will highlight your entire meal!

AVOCADO-CHICKEN SALAD WITH ALMONDS

2 1/2 lb. chicken breasts
1 tbsp. lemon juice
1/3 c. French dressing
1/4 tsp. dry mustard
1 tsp. salt
1/2 tsp. celery salt

1/8 tsp. white pepper
1 c. chopped celery
1 c. diced avocados
1 tbsp. capers
Mayonnaise
1/4 c. salted blanched almonds

Cook the chicken in a small amount of salted water until tender and cool thoroughly in broth. Remove the bones and chop the meat. Combine the chicken, lemon juice, French dressing, mustard and seasonings and toss lightly. Chill for at least 1 hour. Add the celery, avocados, capers and enough mayonnaise to moisten and mix gently. Sprinkle with almonds. Garnish with ripe olives and watercress. 6 servings.

Mrs. James. K. Dowling, Tucson, Arizona

CHICKEN-AVOCADO LUNCHEON SALAD

2 avocados
1 c. cooked diced chicken
3/4 c. diced celery

1/2 c. diced cucumber
1/2 c. mayonnaise
Lettuce or watercress

Cut the avocados in half lengthwise and remove the seeds. Combine the chicken, celery, cucumber and mayonnaise and mix lightly. Heap the chicken mixture in the avocado halves and place on a lettuce leaf. Garnish with lemon wedges. 4 servings.

Wilma Mansel, West Columbia, Texas

CHICKEN-AVOCADO SALAD

2 lge. apples, cubed
1 ripe avocado, cubed
2 tbsp. lemon juice
1/2 c. mayonnaise

1/4 c. cream
1 tsp. minced onion
1/4 c. crumbled bleu cheese
2 c. cubed cooked chicken

Sprinkle the apples and avocado with the lemon juice. Combine the mayonnaise and cream and add the onion. Combine all of the ingredients and toss lightly. Serve on lettuce leaves.

Mrs. Katherine S. Hunter, Irving, Texas

BANANA-CHICKEN SALAD

1 c. sliced bananas
1/2 c. diced pineapple
1 1/2 c. diced cooked chicken
1/2 c. diced celery

1/4 c. sliced olives
1 1/2 tsp. salt
2 tbsp. mayonnaise

Combine the bananas and pineapple and add the chicken, celery, olives, salt and mayonnaise. Mix lightly and serve in lettuce cups. 4-6 servings.

Mrs. G. S. Tramn, Orlando, Florida

TOMATOES STUFFED WITH PINEAPPLE-CHICKEN SALAD

4 c. cubed cooked chicken	Fruit Dressing
2 c. pineapple chunks	8 med. tomatoes
1 c. cubed celery	Lettuce
1/2 c. slivered almonds	Pimento strips
1/2 c. chopped green pepper	Ripe olives

Mix first 5 ingredients in a bowl. Add 1 cup Fruit Dressing and toss well. Cut the tomatoes in sections 3/4 of the way down and stuff with chicken mixture. Serve on lettuce and garnish with remaining Fruit Dressing, pimento strips and olives.

Fruit Dressing

3 tbsp. sugar	2 egg yolks
1/4 c. flour	1/4 c. lemon juice
1/2 tsp. salt	1/3 c. ice water
3/4 c. pineapple juice	1/3 c. instant nonfat dry milk

Mix the sugar, flour and salt in a saucepan. Add the pineapple juice slowly and mix well. Cook over low heat, stirring, until thickened. Beat the egg yolks in a bowl and stir in part of the cooked mixture gradually. Stir back into cooked mixture and cook for 3 minutes. Remove from heat and add the lemon juice. Chill. Mix the water and dry milk in a bowl and whip until stiff. Fold into dressing just before using.

Tomatoes Stuffed with Pineapple-Chicken Salad (above)

BIRD OF PARADISE

3 c. cubed cooked chicken
1 1/2 c. diced celery
1 tsp. salt
3 hard-cooked eggs, chopped
3 sweet pickles, chopped

Mayonnaise to taste
1 fresh pineapple
1 apple
Maraschino cherries

Combine the chicken, celery, salt, eggs and pickles and moisten with mayonnaise. Slice the pineapple in half lengthwise and scoop out the pulp. Cut the pulp in cubes and place in shells. Place the chicken salad on the pineapple cubes to form the body of the birds. Slice the apple in half and attach 1 apple half to each pineapple half with a toothpick, forming head of bird. Attach cherries to apple for eyes. Place on platter of lettuce and garnish with tomato slices and hard-boiled egg wedges. Form the tail of the bird with straws. 2 servings.

Mrs. Richard L. Smith, Tucson, Arizona

BREAST OF CHICKEN SALAD

3 c. cooked chopped chicken
   breast
2 c. coarsely chopped celery
2 tbsp. cream

3/4 c. mayonnaise
1 tbsp. lemon juice
Salt and pepper to taste

Combine all of the ingredients and mix well. Garnish with olives and parsley.

Lillie Mae Edgeston, Ripley, Mississippi

CHICKEN SALAD PIE

2 c. diced cooked chicken
3/4 c. shredded American cheese
1/2 c. diced celery
1/2 c. drained crushed
   pineapple
1/3 c. chopped walnuts

1/2 tsp. paprika
1/2 tsp. salt
3/4 c. mayonnaise
1 baked pie shell
1/2 c. heavy cream

Combine the chicken, cheese, celery, pineapple, walnuts, paprika, salt and 1/2 cup mayonnaise and turn into cooled pie shell. Whip the cream until thick and stiff and fold in remaining mayonnaise carefully. Spread over salad in pie shell. Garnish with grated cheese and chill for at least 30 minutes. 6 servings.

Mrs. Dale Kinney, Greenville, Florida

CHICKEN SALAD WITH EGG DRESSING

2 c. chopped cooked chicken
1 c. diced celery tops
3 hard-boiled eggs

1 egg yolk
1/2 c. olive oil
4 tbsp. vinegar

1 tsp. salt
1/2 tsp. pepper

6 stuffed green olives

Chill the chicken and then mix with the celery. Remove the yolks from the hard-boiled eggs and mash. Add the egg yolk and mix well. Add the oil slowly, beating constantly until thick, then beat in the vinegar, salt and pepper. Chop the egg whites fine and add to the egg yolk mixture. Pour over the cold chicken mixture and mix. Garnish with olives and celery tops and serve.

Mrs. Estelle Shalla, Bay City, Texas

CHICKEN SALAD RING

1 env. unflavored gelatin
2 c. hot chicken broth
1 whole pimento
5 c. diced cooked chicken
3/4 c. finely chopped celery
2 tbsp. chopped sweet pickle

1 tsp. minced green onion
1/2 tsp. crushed rosemary
2 tsp. lemon juice
Salt and pepper to taste
1/3 c. mayonnaise or salad
** dressing**

Soften the gelatin in 1/4 cup water. Add to the hot broth and stir until dissolved. Pour 1/4 cup broth mixture into a 6-cup mold and chill until set. Cut half the pimento into thin strips and place in a pattern on congealed layer. Spoon small amount of cooled broth mixture over pimento and chill until set. Chop remaining pimento and add remaining ingredients except mayonnaise. Add to remaining broth mixture and mix well. Chill until partially set, then fold in the mayonnaise. Place in mold and chill until set. Unmold on serving platter and garnish with radish roses and parsley. Serve with crisp greens and mayonnaise, if desired. 10 servings.

Chicken Salad Ring (above)

CHICKEN-COTTAGE CHEESE SALAD

1 pkg. lime gelatin	1 c. creamed cottage cheese
2 tbsp. lemon juice	1/2 c. diced celery
1/2 tsp. salt	1 c. diced cooked chicken
1/2 c. mayonnaise	1/2 c. finely chopped pickles

Dissolve the gelatin in 1 cup hot water and add 1/2 cup cold water, lemon juice, salt and mayonnaise. Blend well and chill until partially set. Whip until light and fluffy, then fold in remaining ingredients. Place in mold and chill until firm. Unmold and serve on lettuce leaves. 6-8 servings.

Elizabeth Heard, Jackson, Mississippi

LAYERED CHICKEN-CRANBERRY PARTY SALAD

3 env. unflavored gelatin	1/2 c. slivered almonds
2 cans cream of chicken soup	1/2 c. chopped celery
1/4 c. mayonnaise	1 can jellied cranberry sauce
1/2 c. whipped cream	1 tsp. grated lemon peel
1 c. diced cooked chicken	1 tbsp. lemon juice

Soften 2 envelopes of the gelatin in 1/2 cup water. Heat 1 can soup and add to the gelatin, stirring until dissolved. Add the remaining soup and cool. Fold in the mayonnaise, whipped cream, chicken, almonds and celery and pour into greased molds. Chill until firm. Crush the cranberry sauce with a fork. Soften the remaining gelatin in 1/4 cup water and dissolve over hot water, stirring until gelatin dissolves. Add the cranberry sauce, lemon peel and lemon juice and pour over the chilled layer. Chill until firm and serve on crisp salad greens. 6-8 servings.

Mrs. J. M. Christian, Dublin, Georgia

Reception Salad (page 45)

CHICKEN BUFFET MOLDS

1 env. unflavored gelatin	3 tbsp. chopped green olives
1 c. mayonnaise	1 tbsp. chopped pimento
1 1/2 c. diced cooked chicken	2 tbsp. lemon juice
1/2 c. unpared chopped cucumber	1/2 tsp. salt
1/3 c. diced celery	1/4 tsp. paprika
3 tbsp. minced onion	1 c. heavy cream, whipped

Soften the gelatin in 1/2 cup cold water, then dissolve over hot water. Add all the remaining ingredients, folding in the whipped cream last. Pour into individual molds and chill until firm. 8 servings.

Mrs. L. M. Dawson, Tampa, Florida

SALADE DE POULET

1 tbsp. unflavored gelatin	3 hard-cooked eggs, chopped
1 can cream of chicken soup	1/2 c. chopped celery
1/2 c. mayonnaise	1/2 c. chopped cucumber
2 tbsp. prepared horseradish	1/2 c. sliced seeded grapes
1 c. diced cooked chicken	1/2 c. salted pecan halves

Sprinkle the gelatin over 1/2 cup cold water and let stand for 5 minutes. Dissolve over hot water and then stir in the soup, mayonnaise and horseradish. Chill until thick. Mix the remaining ingredients together and chill, then blend into the gelatin mixture. Pour into an oiled mold and chill for 4 hours. 12 servings.

Mrs. Vernelle K. Byrd, Clarkton, North Carolina

RECEPTION SALAD

3 env. unflavored gelatin	2 stalks celery, chopped
1 c. cold water	1/4 c. lemon juice
4 c. tomato juice	1 tsp. onion juice
1 tsp. salt	Chicken Salad
4 peppercorns	Salad greens
1 bay leaf	

Soften the gelatin in cold water. Mix the tomato juice, salt, peppercorns, bay leaf and celery in a saucepan and bring to a boil. Reduce heat and simmer for 10 minutes. Strain. Add softened gelatin to hot liquid and stir until completely dissolved. Mix in the lemon juice and onion juice and pour into twelve 1/2 cup heart-shaped molds. Chill until firm. Unmold onto serving plate. Spoon Chicken Salad on top of each serving and garnish with salad greens. May be poured into 9-inch square pan, chilled and cut with heart-shaped cutter.

Chicken Salad

1/2 lb. chopped cooked chicken	2 tbsp. finely chopped parsley
1 c. finely chopped celery	1/2 c. real mayonnaise

Mix the chicken with remaining ingredients and chill.

CHICKEN JEWEL RING SALAD

2 env. unflavored gelatin	1 c. mayonnaise
1 c. cranberry juice cocktail	1 1/2 c. diced cooked chicken
1 1-lb. can whole cranberry sauce	1/2 c. diced celery
2 tbsp. lemon juice	1/4 c. chopped toasted almonds
1 tbsp. soy sauce	

Sprinkle 1 envelope unflavored gelatin on the cranberry juice cocktail in a sauce-pan to soften. Dissolve gelatin over low heat, stirring constantly. Break up the cranberry sauce and stir into gelatin mixture. Add the lemon juice and pour into a 6-cup ring mold. Chill until almost firm. Sprinkle the remaining gelatin on 3/4 cup cold water in a saucepan to soften and dissolve over low heat, stirring constantly. Remove from heat and stir in the soy sauce. Cool. Stir the gelatin mixture into the mayonnaise gradually until blended, then mix in the remaining ingredients. Spoon over the chilled cranberry layer and chill until firm. Unmold onto salad greens. 8 servings.

Mrs. Cecil Day, Stuttgart, Arkansas

CHICKEN SOUP SALAD

1 env. unflavored gelatin	1 carrot, grated
1 can cream of chicken soup	2 hard-cooked eggs, grated
1 3-oz. package cream cheese	1/2 c. diced celery
1/2 c. mayonnaise	1/4 tsp. salt
Juice of 1 lemon	1 c. diced cooked chicken
1/2 tsp. grated onion	

Soften the gelatin in 1/4 cup water. Bring the soup to a boil and pour over the gelatin, stirring constantly until gelatin is dissolved. Cool. Combine the cream cheese, mayonnaise and lemon juice and mix well, then add to the gelatin mixture. Add the remaining ingredients and chill until firm. 6 servings.

Mrs. H. B. Newton, Hollandale, Mississippi

EAST INDIAN CHICKEN SALAD

1 2-lb. cooked chicken, diced	1/2 c. shredded coconut
1 apple, peeled and diced	1/2 tsp. salt
1 c. diced fresh pineapple	2 tbsp. chicken consomme
1/4 c. white raisins	1 c. mayonnaise
1/3 c. diced dates	1 tbsp. curry powder
2 tbsp. chopped chutney	

Combine the chicken, apple, pineapple, raisins, dates, chutney and coconut and sprinkle with the salt. Mix the consomme into the mayonnaise, stirring until well blended, then stir in the curry powder. Add the mayonnaise mixture to the chicken mixture and stir until well blended. Chill until serving time. 4-6 servings.

Mrs. Gustavo O. Benavides, Knoxville, Tennessee

CURRIED CHICKEN AND GRAPE SALAD

3 c. cooked diced chicken
1 1/2 c. thinly sliced celery
1 c. green seedless grapes
2 tbsp. lemon juice
1 1/4 tsp. salt

1/4 tsp. freshly ground pepper
1 1/2 tsp. curry powder
6 tbsp. mayonnaise
3 tbsp. toasted slivered almonds

Combine all the ingredients and toss lightly. Chill. Serve on lettuce and garnish with almonds.

Lois Pullen, Baton Rouge, Louisiana

CURRIED CHICKEN SALAD

3 c. cubed cooked chicken
1 1/2 c. sliced celery
1/2 c. mayonnaise
1/4 c. sour cream

1 tsp. salt
1/8 tsp. onion salt
Juice of 1 lemon
1 tbsp. curry powder

Combine the chicken and celery. Combine the remaining ingredients and then stir into the chicken mixture. Serve on salad greens and garnish with toasted almonds, avocado slices, sweet red pepper and lime wedges. 4 servings.

Mrs. L. P. Ramage, Richmond, Virginia

MAUNA KEA CHICKEN SALAD

1 lb. chicken breasts
3 to 4 celery tops
1/2 onion, chopped
Salt and pepper to taste
2/3 c. instant rice
1 13-oz. can pineapple chunks

1/2 c. flaked coconut
1 tsp. grated onion
1 c. mayonnaise
1 tbsp. lemon juice
1/2 to 1 tsp. curry powder
1 c. finely chopped celery

Combine the chicken, celery tops, chopped onion, salt, pepper and 1 cup water in a saucepan and cook until chicken is tender. Cool and remove the chicken from the bones and dice. Chill. Cook the rice according to package directions and chill. Drain the pineapple and then combine all the ingredients. Mix well and then chill for 24 hours. Serve in lettuce cups. 8 servings.

Mrs. William Wilcox, Fort Worth, Texas

CHICKEN-FRUIT LUNCHEON SALAD

4 c. cooked diced chicken
2 c. chopped celery
1 c. chopped apples
1 c. drained pineapple chunks
1/2 tsp. salt

1 tbsp. curry powder
1/2 c. chopped toasted almonds
1 c. mayonnaise
2 tbsp. lemon juice

Combine all the ingredients and toss until well combined. Serve on crisp lettuce cups. 10 servings.

Mrs. John I. Loy, Parris Island, South Carolina

DOVER CHICKEN SALAD

1 8-oz. can pineapple chunks	1/2 c. sliced ripe olives
3 c. cooked diced chicken	1/2 c. slivered almonds
1 c. diced celery	

Place the pineapple with the juice in a bowl and add the remaining ingredients. Chill for 1 hour for flavors to blend. Drain off the juice and arrange salad on bed of endive and garnish with mayonnaise. 6-8 servings.

Mrs. Jean Forsgren, Cheraw, South Carolina

MARLBOROUGH CHICKEN SALAD WITH TOPPING

1 5-lb. cooked hen, diced	4 tbsp. Durkee's dressing
1 lge. onion, chopped	2 c. white grapes, halved
3 stalks celery, chopped	1/2 lb. sliced almonds
12 pieces of pickle, chopped	1 tsp. salt
4 hard-cooked eggs, chopped	Pepper to taste
3 c. mayonnaise	Pineapple slices

Combine all the ingredients except the pineapple and mix well. Place pineapple slices on a large serving platter. Mound chicken salad in the center.

Topping

1/2 c. heavy cream, whipped	1/3 c. cranberry sauce
1/2 c. mayonnaise	

Combine all of the ingredients and mix well. Chill. Serve over chicken salad. 15 servings.

Mrs. Ernest S. Gibson, Centenary, South Carolina

HOT CHICKEN SALAD EN CASSEROLE

2 c. diced cooked chicken	1/3 c. chopped green pepper
2 c. chopped celery	2 tbsp. lemon juice
1/2 c. slivered toasted almonds	3/4 c. mayonnaise
2 tbsp. chopped pimento	1/2 c. grated Swiss cheese
2 tbsp. minced onion	1 1/2 c. crushed potato chips
1/2 tsp. salt	

Combine all the ingredients except the cheese and potato chips and mix well. Turn into a buttered 1 1/2-quart casserole and top with the cheese and potato chips. Bake in a 350-degree oven for 25 minutes or until the cheese is melted. 6 servings.

Mrs. E. S. Davis, Jacksonville, Florida

HOT CHICKEN-NUT SALAD

2 c. cooked diced chicken	1 can cream of chicken soup
1 c. diced celery	1 can water chestnuts, sliced
3 hard-cooked eggs, diced	Salt and pepper to taste
1 c. mayonnaise	Crushed potato chips
1 tbsp. lemon juice	

Combine all of the ingredients except the potato chips and mix well. Place in a casserole and cover with the potato chips. Bake at 400 degrees for 20 minutes.

Margaret Hefner Peden, Raeford, North Carolina

CHICKEN SALAD WITH BACON

1 sm. head iceberg lettuce	4 slices crisply fried bacon
1 sm. red pepper, cut in chunks	2 tbsp. wine vinegar
1 cucumber, cut in lge. pieces	6 tbsp. salad oil
1 c. small whole mushrooms	Salt to taste
2 c. cooked chicken pieces	1/4 c. mashed Roquefort cheese
2 hard-boiled eggs, quartered	

Tear the lettuce into large pieces and place in a salad bowl. Add the red pepper, cucumber, mushrooms and chicken and toss lightly. Top with eggs and bacon. Mix remaining ingredients well and serve with salad.

Chicken Salad with Bacon (above)

MUSHROOM-CHICKEN SALAD WITH PECANS

1 4-oz. can button mushrooms	1 c. mayonnaise
4 c. diced cooked chicken	1 c. sour cream
2 c. diced celery	2 tbsp. lemon juice
1/2 c. toasted pecans	1 1/2 tsp. salt
4 slices fried bacon, crumbled	

Drain the mushrooms and combine with the chicken, celery, pecans and bacon in a large bowl. Blend the mayonnaise with the sour cream, lemon juice and salt and add to chicken mixture, tossing lightly until mixed. Chill thoroughly. Serve in crisp lettuce cups and garnish with watercress. 6-8 servings.

Mrs. Ernest Senkel, Cameron, Texas

ROYAL COACH CHICKEN SALAD

3 c. diced cooked chicken	2/3 c. salad dressing
2 lge. unpeeled apples, diced	Salad greens
1 1/2 c. seedless white grapes	1/2 c. toasted slivered almonds
1/2 c. diced celery	

Combine the chicken, apples, grapes and celery in a bowl and add the salad dressing. Toss to mix well, then chill. Turn into bowl lined with salad greens and sprinkle the almonds over the top. 6 servings.

Mrs. Jane Johnson, Orlando, Florida

SESAME CHICKEN SALAD

2 c. green grapes	1/2 c. mayonnaise
3 c. diced cooked chicken	1 tbsp. tarragon vinegar
1 c. cashews	1 tbsp. sugar
2/3 c. sesame seed	1 tsp. salt
1 tbsp. butter	White pepper to taste
1 c. sour cream	

Combine the grapes, chicken and cashews. Saute the sesame seed in the butter until brown and add the remaining ingredients. Mix until smooth and pour over the chicken mixture. Toss lightly until well blended. 10 servings.

Mrs. Howard Boydstun, Hot Springs, Arkansas

POULET SALADE

1 frying-size chicken, salted	1/2 tsp. salt
2 hard-boiled eggs	1/4 tsp. pepper
5 to 6 sweet pickles	1/4 tsp. paprika
1/2 c. mayonnaise	1/4 tsp. onion salt (opt.)
2 tbsp. sour cream	1/2 c. chicken broth
2 tsp. vinegar	

Place the chicken on the rack in a pressure saucepan with 1 cup water and cook for 30 minutes at 10 pounds pressure. Cool and remove the meat from the bones. Chop fine in a blender. Chop the eggs and pickles in the blender and then combine with the chicken. Combine the remaining ingredients and mix together thoroughly. Pour over chicken mixture and blend thoroughly, adding more broth if needed.

Mrs. Howard Burchette, Thurmond, North Carolina

TURKEY SALAD

2 5-oz. cans water chestnuts	1 tbsp. lemon juice
4 c. chopped cooked turkey	2 tsp. curry powder
1 lb. seedless green grapes	1 tbsp. soy sauce
1 c. sliced celery	1 sm. can litchi nuts
1 c. toasted slivered almonds	2 c. pineapple chunks
1 1/2 c. mayonnaise	

Drain the water chestnuts and slice, then combine with the turkey, grapes, celery and almonds. Blend the mayonnaise with the lemon juice, curry powder and soy sauce and then toss with the turkey mixture. Serve the litchi nuts and pineapple chunks separately with the salad. 6 servings.

Mrs. Royce K. Skow, Bethesda, Maryland

CURRIED PINEAPPLE-TURKEY SALAD

2 tsp. curry powder	1 c. thinly sliced celery
1/2 c. cider vinegar	1/4 c. finely chopped green pepper
1 tbsp. sugar	1 c. mayonnaise
1/2 tsp. garlic salt	Garlic-Salted Raisins
1 1-lb. 4 1/2-oz. can pineapple	Chopped egg
chunks	Chopped macadamia nuts
4 c. diced cooked turkey	Toasted coconut chips
1/3 c. finely chopped green onion	

Mix the curry powder, vinegar, sugar and garlic salt in a saucepan and heat to simmering. Cool. Drain the pineapple and add to vinegar mixture. Add the turkey and mix lightly. Chill thoroughly. Add the green onion, celery, green pepper and mayonnaise and mix well. Place in a bowl and serve with Garlic-Salted Raisins and remaining ingredients. 6 servings.

Garlic-Salted Raisins

1 c. dark seedless raisins	Garlic salt to taste
2 tsp. butter	

Saute the raisins in butter in a saucepan for 2 to 3 minutes. Sprinkle with garlic salt and cool.

Photograph for this recipe on page 38.

CRANBERRY-TURKEY SALAD LOAF

2 env. unflavored gelatin	2 tbsp. chopped green pepper
2 1/4 c. turkey broth	2 c. cranberries
1 1/2 tsp. salt	3/4 c. sugar
1 tsp. onion juice	1 tbsp. lemon juice
2 c. diced turkey	1/2 c. chopped apple
1 c. chopped celery	1/4 c. chopped nuts

Soften 1 envelope of the gelatin in 1/4 cup cold broth and heat the remaining broth. Add 1/2 teaspoonful salt, onion juice and softened gelatin, then remove from the heat and stir until dissolved. Cool. Chill until mixture begins to thicken, then add the turkey, 1/2 cup celery and green pepper and mix. Turn into a loaf pan and chill until firm. Cook the cranberries in 1 cup water for about 7 minutes or until the skins pop and then force through a fine sieve. Add the sugar to the juice and simmer for 5 minutes. Soften the remaining gelatin in 1/4 cup water and dissolve in the hot cranberry juice. Add the lemon juice and remaining salt and cool. Chill until the mixture begins to thicken. Fold in the remaining celery, apple and nuts and pour over top of the firm turkey layer. Chill until firm. Unmold onto crisp greens and serve with mayonnaise. 8-10 servings.

Mrs. Esther Sigmund, Laredo, Texas

WILD RICE AND TURKEY SALAD

1/2 lb. wild rice	1 5-oz. can sliced almonds
4 c. cooked chopped turkey	1 c. diced celery
1 c. mayonnaise	2 cans mandarin oranges
1/2 c. French dressing	1 No. 2 can pineapple chunks
Salt to taste	

Cook the rice according to the package directions and cool. Add the turkey, mayonnaise, French dressing, salt, almonds and celery, then chill. Drain the oranges and pineapple and add to the turkey mixture just before serving. Serve on lettuce.

Mrs. Betty Nettles, Walterboro, South Carolina

SEVEN-LAYER CHICKEN SALAD SANDWICH

21 4 x 3 3/4-in. slices bread,	Deviled Ham Filling
crusts trimmed	2 8-oz. packages cream
Softened butter	cheese, softened
Chicken Filling	1/4 c. sour cream

Place 3 slices bread side by side on a serving platter and spread with butter. Spread with 1/4 of the Chicken Filling. Spread another 3 slices bread with butter and place, butter side down, on Chicken Filling. Spread tops of bread with butter and then with half the Deviled Ham Filling. Repeat with 2 more layers of bread and 2/3 of the remaining Chicken Filling. Spread 3 more slices bread with butter and place, butter side down, on Chicken Filling. Spread tops of bread with butter and then with remaining Deviled Ham Filling. Repeat with 1 more layer of bread and remaining Chicken Filling. Butter the last 3 slices of bread and place, butter side down, to form top of loaf. Do not butter tops of these slices. Whip the cream cheese with sour cream and frost sides and top of loaf with cream cheese mixture. Pipe remaining cream cheese mixture on loaf with cake decorating tube. Garnish as desired with strips or slices of sweet gherkins, cherry tomato roses, radish roses, carrot or pimento. Chill. Loaf may be prepared the day before serving without frosting, wrapped in plastic wrap and refrigerated. Frost about 1 hour before serving and refrigerate until serving time.

Chicken Filling

2 c. finely chopped cooked chicken
2/3 c. drained sweet pickle relish

1/2 c. finely chopped pecans
2 tbsp. grated onion
1/2 tsp. curry powder
1/2 c. mayonnaise

Place all ingredients in a bowl and mix well. Chill.

Deviled Ham Filling

1 4 1/2-oz. can deviled ham
1/3 c. drained sweet pickle relish
1/4 c. finely chopped celery

1 tbsp. grated Parmesan cheese
1 tbsp. catsup
1 tbsp. mayonnaise

Place all ingredients in a bowl and mix well. Chill.

Seven-Layer Chicken Salad Sandwich (page 52)

Mexican Shrimp Salad with Peanuts (page 70)

gourmet seafood salads

From the banks off Maryland's coast come succulent crabs . . . from the Gulf Coast waters come shrimp and the small warm-water lobsters . . . from teeming rivers and lakes come perch, bream, catfish, and the black bass Southerners call trout. And all this bounty has been turned into gourmet seafood salads by those innovative homemakers — southern women!

One eye-pleasing salad features Cold Salmon with Cucumber Dressing. The brilliant contrast of pink salmon with white and green cucumber makes this salad an all-time favorite. Another such attractive dish is Tuna Salad in Pepper Cups — the vivid color contrast is a prelude to the mixing of flavors and textures which makes this dish such a treat. Baked Crab Imperial Salad is still another gourmet seafood delight — and might be just the dish you'll want to serve at that next "extra-special" dinner! Or perhaps you'll feature shimmering and elegant Lobster Aspic Parisian . . . Avocado with Shrimp . . . or one of the other seafood salads you'll find recipes for in the section that follows.

These are home-tested, highly acclaimed recipes shared with you by *Southern Living* readers, women whose pride in cooking fine food is matched by their willingness to share their culinary secrets and recipes. Explore these recipes now — and soon you'll be known as a homemaker who prepares elegant gourmet-pleasing seafood salads!

55

MOCK LOBSTER SALAD

1 lge. sliced halibut	1 c. chopped celery
1 onion, sliced	Garlic salt to taste
1 tsp. salt	Pepper to taste
1 can tomato soup	Mayonnaise

Place the halibut, onion, 1 cup water and salt in saucepan and cook for 15 to 20 minutes or until halibut flakes easily. Drain, reserving stock and cool. Flake the halibut and then add the soup and enough reserved stock to cover. Refrigerate overnight. Place the halibut mixture in a sieve and drain for 1 hour. Mash the halibut and stir in the celery, garlic salt, pepper and enough mayonnaise to moisten, mixing well. 4-5 servings.

Mrs. S. W. Stokes, Beaumont, Texas

COLD SALMON WITH CUCUMBER DRESSING

2 med. cucumbers	2 tbsp. vinegar
1/2 c. heavy cream	Dash of hot sauce
1/4 c. mayonnaise	1 can salmon, chilled
1 tsp. salt	

Grate the cucumbers and drain for 15 minutes. Whip the cream until stiff peaks form and then fold in the mayonnaise, salt, vinegar, hot sauce and cucumbers. Drain the salmon and remove the skin and bones. Arrange salmon on lettuce bed and garnish with lemon. Serve with the cucumber dressing. 6 servings.

Mrs. G. B. Sidney, Miami, Florida

DELICIOUS SALMON SALAD

1 env. unflavored gelatin	1/2 c. chopped green peppers
3/4 c. mayonnaise	2 tbsp. sliced olives
1 c. red salmon	1/2 tsp. salt
1/2 c. chopped celery	1/4 tbsp. mild vinegar

Soften the gelatin in 1/4 cup cold water, then stir in 3/4 cup hot water. Chill until thickened, then stir in mayonnaise. Add the remaining ingredients and pour into a mold. Chill until firm. Serve on lettuce and garnish with additional mayonnaise and whole olives.

Mrs. S. M. Harris, Charlottesville, Virginia

SALMON-COTTAGE CHEESE SALAD

2 tbsp. sugar	1/4 c. vinegar
2 tsp. salt	1 tbsp. butter
1 tsp. mustard	1 1-lb. can salmon
1 1/2 tbsp. flour	3/4 c. chopped sweet pickle
1 egg, slightly beaten	1/2 c. chopped celery
3/4 c. milk	1 1/4 c. cottage cheese

Combine the sugar, 1 teaspoon salt, mustard, flour, egg and milk in top of a double boiler and blend thoroughly. Stir in the vinegar gradually and cook over hot water, stirring constantly, for about 10 minutes or until thick. Remove from heat and add the butter, stirring to blend. Chill. Drain the salmon and remove the skin and bones, then flake. Add all the remaining ingredients and mix lightly. Add 1/2 cup of the chilled dressing and mix until well blended. Chill. Serve on salad greens and garnish with radish roses, carrot sticks, sliced hard-boiled eggs or cucumber slices. 6 servings.

Bonnie Butts, San Antonio, Texas

MACARONI-SALMON SALAD BOWL

Salt	1 c. chopped celery
3 qt. boiling water	1 c. mayonnaise
2 c. elbow macaroni	1/2 tsp. pepper
1 15-oz. can salmon	1 1/2 tsp. dillweed
1 c. seeded diced cucumber	Chilled lettuce
1/2 c. chopped green pepper	2 hard-cooked eggs, quartered
1/2 c. chopped onion	

Add 1 tablespoon salt to boiling water and add macaroni gradually so that water continues to boil. Cook, stirring occasionally, until tender, then drain in a colander. Rinse with cold water and drain again. Drain the salmon and remove skin and center bone. Flake slightly. Toss the salmon with macaroni, vegetables, mayonnaise, 1 teaspoon salt, pepper and dillweed in a large bowl and cover. Chill thoroughly. Spoon into lettuce-lined bowl and garnish with egg. Sprinkle with additional dillweed, if desired. 4-6 servings.

Macaroni-Salmon Salad Bowl (above)

CONTINENTAL TUNA SALAD

6 cucumbers	1/2 c. chopped celery
1 lge. can tuna	1/4 c. olive oil
1 onion, minced	3 tbsp. cider vinegar
1 c. diced cooked potatoes	1 tsp. capers
3 hard-cooked eggs, diced	1/2 tsp. salt
1/2 green pepper, minced	1/4 tsp. pepper

Cut the cucumbers in half lengthwise and hollow out the centers. Place in ice water until ready to serve. Mix the tuna with onion, potatoes, eggs, green pepper and celery. Mix the remaining ingredients for the salad dressing. Combine the tuna mixture with the dressing and fill the cucumber halves. Serve on crisp lettuce leaves and garnish with pimento-stuffed olives and sprigs of parsley.

Mrs. Forest Cruse, Austin, Texas

TUNA GUACAMOLE SALAD

1/2 c. mashed ripe avocado	1/4 tsp. hot sauce
1/2 c. sour cream	1/2 med. head lettuce
1 clove of garlic, crushed	2 tomatoes, cut in wedges
1/2 tsp. chili powder	1/2 c. sliced ripe olives
1 tbsp. lemon juice	1/4 c. chopped green onions
1/3 c. salad oil	1 can tuna, drained
1/2 tsp. sugar	1 c. corn chips
1/4 tsp. salt	1/2 c. shredded Cheddar cheese

Combine the first 9 ingredients for the dressing and beat with an electric mixer until well blended. Break the lettuce into a bowl and add the tomatoes, olives and onions. Add the tuna, corn chips and dressing, then toss lightly. Sprinkle with the cheese and garnish with olives. 4-6 servings.

Mrs. Harold Dalbom, Clovis, New Mexico

PATIO TUNA BOWL

1/2 lb. fresh string beans	1 2-oz. can anchovies
3 hard-cooked eggs	1 can tuna
2 green peppers	3 tbsp. olive oil
2 lge. tomatoes	1 tbsp. wine vinegar
1 med. onion, sliced	Salt and pepper to taste
8 ripe olives, pitted	

Cook the green beans, uncovered, for 20 minutes in rapidly boiling salted water, then drain and cool. Cut 1 egg into slices and quarter the remaining eggs. Cut the green peppers into thin strips and cut the tomatoes into wedges. Combine the beans, eggs, green peppers, onion, tomatoes and olives. Drain the anchovies and rinse, then add with the tuna to the bean mixture. Combine the olive oil and vinegar and pour over the salad. Toss lightly and season. 4 servings.

Mrs. James J. Gibbons, Lexington, Kentucky

KIDNEY BEAN-TUNA SALAD

1 1-lb. can red kidney beans	1/4 tsp. pepper
1 7-oz. can chunk tuna	1 1/2 tsp. salt
6 anchovy fillets, quartered	1 1/2 tsp. basil leaves
1 c. sliced celery	1 tsp. vinegar
2 tbsp. instant minced onion	1/4 c. mayonnaise
1/4 tsp. instant minced garlic	

Drain the beans and tuna and then combine all ingredients. Mix lightly and chill for at least 1 hour. Serve on lettuce and garnish with tomato wedges. 6 servings.

Mrs. P. E. Bryan, Muskogee, Oklahoma

BUFFET TUNA SALAD

1 sm. head lettuce	6 scallions
2 6 1/2 or 7-oz. cans tuna	12 radishes
in vegetable oil	12 carrot sticks
3 hard-cooked eggs, halved	12 ripe olives
3 whole pimentos	12 cucumber slices
6 green pepper rings	

Cover a large platter with lettuce and place the tuna in center. Surround with remaining ingredients. 6 servings.

Tangy Tuna Dressing

1/2 c. mayonnaise	1 tsp. lemon juice
1/2 tsp. salt	2 tsp. Worcestershire sauce

Blend the mayonnaise, salt, lemon juice and Worcestershire sauce in a bowl. Serve with salad.

Buffet Tuna Salad (above)

TUNA SALAD IN PEPPER CUPS

6 med. green peppers	2 tbsp. chopped pimento
Salt to taste	3/4 c. mayonnaise
3/4 c. instant rice	Dash of pepper
1 can tuna	1/3 c. finely crushed potato
1/2 c. chopped celery	chips
2 tbsp. finely chopped onion	

Cut the green peppers into halves lengthwise and remove the stems and seed. Cook in small amount of boiling, salted water for 5 minutes. Drain and sprinkle insides lightly with salt. Prepare the rice according to package directions and combine with the tuna, celery, onion and pimento. Blend in the mayonnaise, salt and pepper and toss lightly. Spoon the salad mixture into the green pepper halves and sprinkle with potato chips. Place green peppers in a 10 x 6 x 1 1/2-inch baking dish and barely cover bottom of the pan with water. Bake at 350 degrees for 35 minutes. 6 servings.

Mrs. Creel A. Pickel, Dallas, Texas

MOLDED EGG AND TUNA SALAD

1 env. sour cream sauce mix	1 7-oz. can flaked tuna,
1/2 c. milk	drained
2 tsp. prepared mustard	1/2 c. finely diced celery
1/2 tsp. onion salt	1 tbsp. chopped pimento
1 tbsp. unflavored gelatin	2 tbsp. chopped sweet pickle
3 hard-cooked eggs	Pimento strips
2 tbsp. mayonnaise	Crisp lettuce

Place the sauce mix in a bowl and add the milk slowly, stirring constantly. Blend in the mustard and onion salt and let stand for 10 minutes. Soften the gelatin in 1/4 cup cold water, then dissolve over hot water. Dice 2 eggs and add to mustard mixture. Add the mayonnaise, gelatin, tuna, celery, chopped pimento and pickle and mix well. Circle bottom of custard or muffin cups with pimento strips and fill cups with tuna mixture. Chill. Unmold on lettuce leaves. Slice remaining egg and garnish salads with egg slices and additional mayonnaise.

Mrs. Rudell Harville, Alamo, Georgia

MOLDED TUNA SALAD WITH CUCUMBER DRESSING

2 env. unflavored gelatin	1 c. finely diced celery
1 can cream of mushroom soup	1 sm. jar pimento, diced
1 7-oz. can light chunk tuna,	1 sm. onion, grated
drained	1 c. mayonnaise
1 pt. cottage cheese	Salt to taste

Soften the gelatin in 1/2 cup cold water. Heat the soup in a saucepan. Add the gelatin and stir until dissolved. Cool, then fold in remaining ingredients. Spoon into a lightly oiled fish mold and refrigerate for 24 hours. Unmold onto a serving dish and garnish with crisp greens.

Cucumber Dressing

1/2 c. whipped cream
1/4 c. mayonnaise
1 tbsp. lemon juice

1/4 tsp. salt
1/4 tsp. paprika
1 c. diced drained cucumbers

Mix the whipped cream, mayonnaise, lemon juice, salt and paprika in a bowl and fold in the cucumbers. Serve with tuna salad.

Mrs. John Pace, Bristol, Virginia

TUNA POLYNESIAN PLATTER

3/4 c. seedless raisins
3 6 1/2 or 7-oz. cans tuna
   in vegetable oil
1 c. chopped celery
3/4 c. flaked coconut
1/2 c. toasted slivered almonds
1/2 c. mayonnaise
2 tbsp. lemon juice
1 tsp. soy sauce

1/2 tsp. nutmeg
1/4 tsp. ginger
Salad greens
Pineapple slices
Peach halves
Pear halves
Figs
Apricots

Place the raisins in a saucepan and cover with water. Bring to a boil. Remove from heat and let stand for 5 minutes. Drain. Combine the tuna, celery, coconut, raisins and almonds in a bowl. Blend the mayonnaise with lemon juice, soy sauce, nutmeg and ginger and toss lightly with tuna mixture. Chill. Pile the tuna salad on greens in center of a platter and arrange fruits around tuna salad. Garnish tuna salad with additional coconut and almonds, if desired. 6-8 servings.

Tuna Polynesian Platter (above)

TUNA-STUFFED TOMATOES

1 7-oz. can light tuna	1 tbsp. sweet pickle relish
1/2 c. diced celery	Salt and pepper to taste
1/2 c. chopped cucumber	1/4 c. mayonnaise
1 tbsp. minced onion	4 tomatoes
1 tsp. lemon juice	

Combine the tuna, celery, cucumber, onion, lemon juice, relish, salt and pepper, then toss together. Add the mayonnaise and mix lightly until blended. Cut the tops off tomatoes and scoop out the centers. Fill with the tuna salad and serve on lettuce. 4 servings.

Mrs. Howard Riley, Shelby, North Carolina

TUNA STAR SALAD

1 env. unflavored gelatin	1/2 c. diced celery
1 can tomato soup	1/2 c. chopped onion
1 8-oz. package cream cheese	1/4 c. drained pickle relish
1 c. salad dressing	1 can tuna, drained
1/2 c. diced green pepper	

Soften the gelatin in 1/2 cup cold water. Heat the soup in a saucepan. Cut the cream cheese in cubes and add to soup. Heat, beating with rotary beater, until smooth. Add the gelatin and stir until dissolved. Remove from heat and stir in the salad dressing. Chill until partially set. Add remaining ingredients and mix well. Pour into a 5 1/2-cup star mold and chill until set. Unmold on lettuce and garnish with stars cut from pimento. 8 servings.

Mrs. Callie Henderson, New Brockton, Alabama

BEACHCOMBER SALAD

1 can tomato soup	1/2 tsp. minced onion
1 6-oz. can minced clams	1 tsp. lemon juice
1 8-oz. package cream cheese	1/8 tsp. pepper
2 env. unflavored gelatin	Salt to taste
3/4 c. mayonnaise	Dash of paprika
1 c. chopped celery	Worcestershire sauce to taste
2 hard-cooked eggs, chopped	4 stuffed green olives, sliced
6 stuffed green olives, chopped	

Pour the tomato soup in a saucepan. Drain the clams and reserve liquor. Add enough water to reserved liquor to make 1 soup can liquid and stir into soup. Bring to a boil. Add the cream cheese and simmer, stirring, until cheese is partially melted. Remove from heat and beat with rotary beater until thoroughly blended. Soften the gelatin in 1/2 cup cold water. Add to the hot soup mixture and stir until dissolved. Cool, then chill until thickened. Stir in remaining ingredients except sliced olives. Decorate bottom of a 1 1/2-quart mold with sliced olives. Spoon clam mixture into mold and chill until firm. Unmold onto salad greens.

Anna Hall, Springfield, Virginia

WEST INDIES SALAD

1 med. onion, finely chopped	1/2 c. salad oil
1 lb. fresh lump crab meat	6 tbsp. cider vinegar
Salt and pepper to taste	1/2 c. ice water

Place half the onion in a bowl. Place the crab meat on onion and spread remaining onion over crab meat. Season with salt and pepper. Pour oil, then vinegar, then ice water over onion. Cover and refrigerate until chilled. Toss lightly just before serving. 6 servings.

Grace Lunsford, Foley, Alabama

CRAB SALAD

1 sm. head iceberg lettuce	1 sm. red pepper, cut in
1 lb. crab meat	chunks
2 tomatoes, chopped	4 green onions, cut in strips
1 sm. green pepper, cut in	Italian dressing
chunks	

Tear the lettuce into bite-sized pieces. Place the crab meat, lettuce, tomatoes, green and red peppers and onions in a bowl and toss lightly. Serve on individual plates with Italian dressing. 4 servings.

Crab Salad (above)

CAPER-CRAB MEAT SALAD

6 med. tomatoes	6 tbsp. mayonnaise
6 tbsp. French dressing	1/4 c. capers
2 c. flaked crab meat	Paprika
1/2 c. diced celery	Watercress

Scald, peel and chill the tomatoes. Scoop out centers to form cups. Pour 1 tablespoon French dressing into each tomato cup and marinate in refrigerator for 30 minutes. Drain the tomatoes and reserve French dressing. Mix the crab meat, celery and reserved French dressing gently. Stuff tomatoes with crab meat mixture. Place 1 tablespoon mayonnaise on each tomato and garnish with capers and paprika. Serve on watercress.

Patricia A. Glass, Dill City, Oklahoma

BAKED CRAB IMPERIAL SALAD

1 c. mayonnaise	Dash of pepper
1/4 c. finely chopped onion	2 c. crab meat, drained
1/4 c. finely chopped green pepper	2 hard-cooked eggs, chopped
	4 med. avocados
1/2 tsp. dry mustard	1 c. soft bread crumbs
3 tbsp. lemon juice	2 tbsp. melted butter
1/2 tsp. salt	

Combine the mayonnaise, onion, green pepper, mustard, 2 tablespoons lemon juice, salt and pepper in a bowl. Add the crab meat and eggs and mix well. Cut avocados into halves and remove seeds. Brush cut surfaces with remaining lemon juice and mound crab mixture on avocado halves. Combine the bread crumbs and butter and sprinkle over crab mixture. Place in a baking pan. Bake at 350 degrees for 10 to 15 minutes or until crumbs are lightly browned. Serve at once.

Mrs. William E. Perry, Statesville, North Carolina

CRAB LOUIS

3 6 1/2-oz. cans crab meat, flaked	1/2 c. chili sauce
6 c. shredded lettuce	2 tbsp. horseradish
2 hard-cooked eggs, diced	4 tsp. lemon juice
2 tbsp. chopped onion or chives	1 tsp. salt
1 1/3 c. mayonnaise	1/4 tsp. pepper
1/3 c. heavy cream	3/4 tsp. Worcestershire sauce

Combine the crab meat, lettuce, eggs and onion in a large salad bowl. Combine the mayonnaise, cream, chili sauce, horseradish, lemon juice, salt, pepper and Worcestershire sauce and mix well. Pour over crab meat mixture and toss lightly. Garnish with tomato wedges. 6 servings.

Mrs. May Round, Laurel, Mississippi

CRAB-PEAR SALAD WITH HOT VINAIGRETTE DRESSING

1 7 1/2-oz. can Alaska King crab, drained	1/4 tsp. garlic powder
1 c. chopped celery	1 tbsp. chopped chives
2 hard-cooked eggs, chopped	1/2 c. salad oil
1/4 tsp. dry mustard	2 tbsp. vinegar
1 tsp. salt	2 tbsp. fresh lemon juice
1/8 tsp. pepper	1 1-lb. 13-oz. can Bartlett pear halves, drained

Mix the crab with celery and eggs in a bowl. Blend the mustard with salt, pepper, garlic powder, chives, oil, vinegar and lemon juice in a saucepan and heat to boiling point. Add the pear halves and simmer for 5 minutes. Remove pears to a platter. Pour hot sauce over crab mixture and toss lightly. Heap crab mixture in center of platter. Garnish with crisp celery greens. 4 servings.

Mrs. William R. Swift, Bowling Green, Kentucky

CRAB-STUFFED AVOCADO

1/2 c. mayonnaise	Dash of hot sauce
1/2 c. minced celery	2 ripe avocados
1/4 c. minced pimento	Lettuce
Lemon juice	1 1/2 c. crab meat
1/8 tsp. Worcestershire sauce	Salt to taste

Combine the mayonnaise, celery, pimento, 2 teaspoons lemon juice, Worcestershire sauce and hot sauce in a bowl. Cut avocados lengthwise, then remove seeds and peel. Dip in lemon juice. Arrange lettuce on 4 salad plates and place avocado halves on lettuce. Fill with crab meat and sprinkle with salt. Spoon mayonnaise mixture over top. 4 servings.

Jessie A. Silva, El Paso, Texas

HOT CRAB SALAD BOATS

1 lb. lump crab meat	3/4 c. mayonnaise
1 c. diced celery	6 long hero-type rolls
1 c. cooked peas	1/4 c. melted margarine
1/4 lb. Swiss process cheese, cubed	6 lemon wedges
1/4 c. chopped parsley	12 ripe olives

Combine the crab meat, celery, peas, cheese and parsley in a bowl and fold in the mayonnaise. Cut a slice from top of each roll and remove center to make a boat-shaped shell. Brush inside of shells with butter and fill with crab meat mixture. Wrap each separately in foil and place on a baking sheet. Bake at 400 degrees for 15 minutes. Thread 6 toothpicks with 1 lemon wedge and 2 olives each and place on boats.

Mrs. Joseph B. Medagliani, Halifax, Virginia

King Crab-Celery Victor (below)

KING CRAB-CELERY VICTOR

2 6-oz. packages frozen or fresh King crab meat	3 c. boiling water
2 celery hearts	1 c. low-calorie French dressing
2 chicken bouillon cubes	3 lge. lettuce cups
	Pepper to taste

Thaw frozen crab meat. Drain the crab meat and remove any shell or cartilage. Cut crab meat into 1-inch pieces and chill. Wash and trim the celery hearts to 5-inch lengths. Cut each heart in thirds lengthwise and place in a 10-inch frypan. Dissolve the bouillon cubes in boiling water and pour over celery. Cover and simmer for 10 to 15 minutes or until celery is tender. Cool, then drain. Place the celery in a shallow dish and add the French dressing. Chill for at least 2 hours. Drain the celery and place in lettuce cups. Place the crab meat over celery and sprinkle with pepper. Garnish with green olives if desired. Two 6 1/2 or 7 1/2-ounce cans crab meat may be substituted for King crab.

CRAB AND OLIVE SALAD

2 6 1/2-oz. cans crab meat	1/4 c. mayonnaise or salad dressing
2/3 c. chopped ripe olives	Salt and pepper to taste
1 2/3 c. diced celery	Romaine

Flake the crab meat and remove shell and cartilage. Place in a bowl. Add the olives, celery, mayonnaise, salt and pepper and mix well. Serve on romaine.

Mrs. Geneva Bryant, Jacksonville, Arkansas

LOBSTER ASPIC PARISIAN

3 env. unflavored gelatin	1 1/2 c. cooked peas
1 1/3 c. cold water	1 c. diced cooked carrots
2 cans bouillon, heated	1 1/2 c. diced cooked potatoes
2 tbsp. lemon juice	2 tsp. salt
2 tsp. Worcestershire sauce	2/3 c. mayonnaise
1 1/2 lb. cooked lobster	

Soften the gelatin in water and dissolve in bouillon. Stir in the lemon juice and Worcestershire sauce and chill until thickened. Pour 1 cup gelatin mixture into a 4-cup mold and arrange pieces of lobster, red side down, in gelatin mixture. Chill until almost set. Dice remaining lobster and stir in the peas, carrots, potatoes, salt and mayonnaise. Add to remaining gelatin mixture and spoon into the mold. Chill until firm. Unmold onto lettuce and garnish with wedges of tomato, hard-cooked eggs, ripe olives or lemon wedges, if desired. 8-10 servings.

Mrs. James B. Miller, Santa Fe, New Mexico

LOBSTER-ORANGE SALAD PUFFS

2 c. cubed cooked lobster	1 c. sour cream
2 c. diced orange	1/4 c. mayonnaise
1/4 c. minced green onions	1 1/2 tsp. salt
2 tbsp. minced parsley	1 tsp. hot sauce

Combine the lobster, orange, onions and parsley. Combine the sour cream, mayonnaise, salt and hot sauce and blend well. Add to lobster mixture and mix well. Chill.

Puff Shells

1 c. water	Dash of salt
1/2 c. butter or margarine	4 eggs
1 c. sifted flour	

Bring the water and butter to a boil in a heavy saucepan, stirring until butter melts. Add flour and salt all at once and reduce heat. Cook and stir for 1 to 2 minutes or until mixture forms a ball. Remove from heat and cool slightly. Add the eggs, one at a time, beating well after each addition. Drop by rounded tablespoonfuls onto a lightly greased baking sheet. Bake at 400 degrees for 40 to 45 minutes or until firm, then cool. Cut off tops of shells and scoop out insides. Fill with lobster mixture and refrigerate until chilled. 8 servings.

Mrs. Lloyd Sorenson, Columbus, Mississippi

Walnut-Lobster Salad Cantonese (below)

WALNUT-LOBSTER SALAD CANTONESE

1 5-oz. can water chestnuts	1 c. diagonally sliced celery
1 11-oz. can mandarin orange	1/2 c. sliced green onions
segments	3 c. cooked lobster chunks
1 tbsp. butter	Sweet-Sour Dressing
1 tbsp. soy sauce	Crisp watercress or salad greens
1 c. large walnut pieces and halves	

Drain and slice the water chestnuts. Drain the orange segments. Melt butter in a saucepan and add the soy sauce and walnuts. Stir gently over low heat for about 10 minutes or until walnuts are lightly toasted. Remove from heat and cool. Combine the celery, green onions, water chestnuts, orange segments and lobster in a bowl and add just enough Sweet-Sour Dressing to hold ingredients together. Fold in the walnuts. Place on watercress on a serving dish and serve with remaining Sweet-Sour Dressing, if desired. Prawns, crab or tuna may be substituted for lobster. 6 servings.

Sweet-Sour Dressing

3 eggs	1/3 c. strained lemon juice
1/2 c. sugar	1/3 c. cider vinegar
2 tbsp. all-purpose flour	1 14 1/2-oz. can evaporated milk
2 tsp. seasoned salt	1 tbsp. soft or melted butter
1/8 tsp. curry powder	

Beat the eggs in top of a double boiler, then beat in sugar, flour, salt and curry powder. Blend in the lemon juice and vinegar. Cook over boiling water for about 10 minutes or until thickened, stirring frequently to keep smooth. Beat in undiluted evaporated milk and butter and cool. Store in covered container in refrigerator. About 3 cups.

LOBSTER SALAD TROPICALE

1 c. diced cooked lobster	1 peeled avocado, sliced
1 peeled grapefruit, sectioned	1/2 c. slivered toasted almonds

1/2 c. mayonnaise   Salt to taste
1 tsp. horseradish   Mixed salad greens
Dash of cayenne pepper

Place the lobster, grapefruit, avocado and almonds in a bowl and mix lightly. Mix the mayonnaise, horseradish, cayenne pepper and salt and fold into lobster mixture. Serve on greens. 4 servings.

Mrs. J. E. Swaim, Jr., England, Arkansas

AVOCADO WITH SHRIMP

2 med. avocados, pared   2 hard-cooked eggs, chopped
Lemon juice   2 tbsp. mayonnaise
Shredded lettuce   2 hard-cooked eggs, sliced
20 shrimp   Stuffed olives
1/2 c. chopped celery

Cut the avocados in half lengthwise and remove seeds. Sprinkle with lemon juice and place on lettuce. Combine the shrimp, celery and chopped eggs and stir in mayonnaise. Place on avocado halves and garnish with egg slices and olives.

Mrs. K. C. Hawkins, Arkadelphia, Arkansas

MARINATED SHRIMP SALAD

4 lb. cooked shrimp   1 c. mayonnaise
2 tbsp. lemon juice   1 c. melon balls
1/2 tbsp. grated onion   1/2 c. chopped celery
1 1/2 tbsp. salt   1/2 c. pineapple chunks
1 1/2 tbsp. curry powder   French dressing
6 tbsp. sour cream

Combine the shrimp, lemon juice, onion and salt in a bowl and chill overnight. Mix the curry powder, sour cream and mayonnaise and chill for several hours. Marinate the melon balls, celery and pineapple chunks in small amount of French dressing in refrigerator for several hours, then drain. Mix the shrimp mixture, sour cream mixture and pineapple mixture and serve. 8 servings.

Mrs. S. A. Chandler, Meridian, Mississippi

SHRIMP HAWAIIAN

1 5-oz. can water chestnuts   2 5-oz. cans shrimp, drained
1 14-oz. can pineapple chunks   1/2 c. mayonnaise
6 c. torn salad greens   1/4 c. crumbled Roquefort cheese

Drain and chop the water chestnuts. Drain the pineapple, reserving 2 tablespoons syrup. Place the salad greens in a large bowl and add the shrimp, pineapple chunks and water chestnuts. Blend reserved pineapple syrup with mayonnaise and cheese and pour over shrimp mixture. Toss lightly to mix. 6 servings.

Mrs. J. R. Pennington, Myrtle Beach, South Carolina

MEXICAN SHRIMP SALAD WITH PEANUTS

2/3 c. peanut oil	5 sm. heads Bibb lettuce, quartered
2 tbsp. white vinegar	1 1/2 lb. small cooked shrimp,
2 tbsp. orange juice	cleaned
2 tbsp. finely chopped chutney	3 lge. peeled oranges, sectioned
1 clove of garlic, crushed	2 med. peeled red onions,
1 tsp. salt	thinly sliced
1 tsp. curry powder	1 green pepper, sliced in strips
1/4 tsp. hot sauce	2/3 c. cocktail peanuts

Combine the peanut oil, vinegar, orange juice, chutney, garlic, salt, curry powder and hot sauce in a jar and cover. Shake well. Place the lettuce, shrimp, orange sections, onions, green pepper and peanuts in a salad bowl and toss. Shake the dressing and pour over salad mixture. Toss lightly and serve immediately. 6 servings.

Photograph for this recipe on page 54.

NEW ORLEANS SHRIMP SALAD

1/2 c. rice	6 stuffed olives, sliced
1 4 1/2-oz. can shrimp, drained	Juice of 1 lemon
1/2 green pepper, finely chopped	Salt and pepper to taste
1 sm. onion, finely chopped	Dash of hot sauce
1 c. cauliflowerets	1/4 to 1/2 c. mayonnaise

Cook the rice in boiling, salted water until tender. Drain and cool. Combine the shrimp, rice, green pepper, onion, cauliflowerets, olives, lemon juice, salt, pepper, hot sauce and mayonnaise and mix well. Chill for at least 4 hours. 4 servings.

Mrs. Frank L. Jones, Alexandria, Louisiana

SHRIMP BOWL WITH PIQUANT DRESSING

1 head iceberg lettuce	12 stuffed olives, sliced
1/4 head curly lettuce	Piquant Dressing
1 lb. peeled cooked shrimp	2 hard-cooked eggs, sliced

Cut the lettuce into bite-sized pieces and chill. Chill the shrimp. Combine the lettuce, shrimp and olives in a salad bowl. Add the Piquant Dressing and toss lightly. Garnish with eggs. 4-6 servings.

Piquant Dressing

1 c. cold evaporated milk	3 tbsp. prepared mustard
1 tbsp. lemon juice	1/2 tsp. salt
1 tbsp. chopped chives	1/4 tsp. cayenne pepper

Blend the evaporated milk and lemon juice in a mixing bowl. Stir in remaining ingredients and chill.

Mrs. Nina T. Smith, Picayune, Mississippi

SHRIMP SALAD BOAT

1 loaf Italian bread
4 hard-cooked eggs, diced
1 c. chopped shrimp
1 c. diced celery
2 tbsp. chopped dill pickle
2 tbsp. chopped stuffed olives

1 tbsp. minced scallions
1/2 tsp. garlic salt
1/4 tsp. dry mustard
1/2 c. mayonnaise
2 tbsp. melted butter

Cut off top of loaf of bread and remove center to leave a 1-inch thick shell. Crumble bread removed from loaf and reserve 1 cup crumbs. Combine reserved crumbs with remaining ingredients except butter and spoon into loaf shell. Replace top. Brush entire loaf with butter and wrap in aluminum foil. Place on a cookie sheet. Bake at 450 degrees for 30 minutes. Cut in 6 slices and serve at once. Chicken, ham or tuna may be substituted for shrimp. 6 servings.

Mrs. R. C. Lewis, Augusta, Georgia

CURRIED SHRIMP SALAD

2 1-lb. packages frozen peeled
    deveined shrimp
2 tsp. salt
Juice of 1/2 lemon
1 bay leaf
2 or 3 whole peppercorns
1 c. mayonnaise

2 tsp. curry powder
2 tsp. soy sauce
3 tbsp. minced green onion
1/2 c. minced celery
Cherry tomatoes
Whole ripe olives

Cook the shrimp according to package directions, adding salt, lemon juice, bay leaf and peppercorns. Drain and cool, then chill. Mix the mayonnaise, curry powder and soy sauce in a bowl and chill. Combine the shrimp, green onion and celery in a bowl. Add mayonnaise mixture and toss lightly. Garnish with tomatoes and olives. Dash of pepper may be substituted for peppercorns. 6-8 servings.

Curried Shrimp Salad (above)

Walnut Antipasto Salad (page 80)

vegetable salads

For low cost . . . high nutritional value . . . and delicious variety in flavor and color, vegetable salads are unexcelled. When you are serving the traditional roast beef and potatoes dinner, you know you can depend on a tossed salad to introduce variety in color and texture. And when the main dish is a casserole, an aspic or congealed vegetable salad offers pleasant contrast.

Southern women, who are noted for the careful planning that goes into their meals, know the many values vegetable salads offer – and they have been developing great salad recipes for years. Now the very best of these recipes have been brought together and are shared with you in the section that follows.

Feature asparagus in Autumn Garden Salad – then sit back and listen to the compliments flow! Highlight those meals which need a crispy, crunchy flavor with Cream Coleslaw – bright cabbage with an inimitable dressing. And don't forget California Caesar Salad – everyone's favorite, suitable for an appetizer or an entree in a salad bowl. Potato Salad receives a new treatment when it's served as Hot German Potato Salad – an import that is a favorite with southern families.

There are many more vegetable salads awaiting your discovery in the pages that follow. Explore – then delight your family and guests by serving a salad – soon!

73

Crisp and crunchy vegetable salads — for eye-appeal, flavor, and nutritional value, they're just about unbeatable. But even the best salads become commonplace when they're served every day. To perk them up, try adding just a pinch of herbs. The best proportion is about 1/4 teaspoon of herbs per four servings, and the most successful way to use them is in the dressing you add to your vegetable salad.

Dried herbs should be crushed before mixing them into the salad. If you are using fresh ones, mince them before combining with the dressing. You'll want to use three to four times as much fresh herbs as you do dried.

The basic herbs for salads are basil — particularly good with tomatoes, cucumbers, and beans; marjoram — marvelous with tomatoes and spinach; parsley — an attractive decoration as well as a flavorful herb; and tarragon —

general directions
FOR VEGETABLE SALADS

frequently featured in salad vinegars. By experimenting with these and other herbs, you'll be able to create an infinite variety of salads to please your family and guests.

Another way to vary salads is with garnishes. Grated cheese . . . parsley sprigs . . . sliced hard-cooked eggs . . . crumbled bleu cheese . . . nuts . . . mushrooms . . . and fried onion rings are all attractive garnishes which can bring new notes of color, flavor, and texture to your salads.

Even when you dress them up, most vegetable salads are remarkably low in calories. The following chart gives calorie values for normal portions of vegetables frequently used in salads:

VEGETABLE CALORIE CHART		
VEGETABLE	**AMOUNT**	**CALORIES**
ASPARAGUS	1 cup	35
BAMBOO SHOOTS, canned	1/2 cup	30
BEANS: baby lima green navy red kidney wax or yellow	1 cup 1 cup 1 cup 1 cup 1 cup	150 25 230 230 25
BEAN SPROUTS	1 cup	20
BEET GREENS	1 cup	40

VEGETABLE CALORIE CHART

VEGETABLE	AMOUNT	CALORIES
BEETS	1 cup	70
BROCCOLI	1 cup	45
BRUSSELS SPROUTS	1 cup	60
CABBAGE:		
cooked	1 cup	40
raw, shredded	1 cup	25
CARROTS:		
cooked	1 cup	45
raw	one	20
grated	1 cup	45
CAULIFLOWER:		
cooked	1 cup	30
raw	1 cup	25
CELERY:		
cooked	1 cup	24
raw	1 cup	20
one large stalk	8" long	5
COLESLAW	1 cup	100
CUCUMBER:		
6 slices, pared		5
one cucumber, raw, pared		25
ENDIVE	1 pound	80
ESCAROLE	1 pound	80
LETTUCE:		
one head, compact		70
one head, loose-leaf		30
2 large or 4 small leaves		5
MUSHROOMS, canned	1 cup	30
OLIVES, extra-large:		
green	12	65
ripe	12	80
ONIONS:		
cooked	1 cup	80
raw	one, 2½" diameter	50
raw	1 tbsp., chopped	5
young green	6 small	25
PARSLEY	1 tbsp., chopped	1
PEAS:		
canned	1 cup	170
cooked	1 cup	110
PEPPERS, green	1 medium	15
PICKLES:		
dill	1 large	15
sweet	one	20
PIMIENTOS, canned	1 medium	10
POTATOES:		
boiled	1 cup diced or 1 medium, 2½" diameter	105
canned	3-4, small	120
RADISHES, raw	four	10
RICE	1 cup	200
SPINACH, cooked	1 cup	45
TOMATOES:		
canned or cooked	1 cup	45
raw	1 medium, 2" x 2½"	30

American homemakers are fortunate in having a number of different salad vegetables to choose from. Some are available only during certain times of the year while others are grown year-round. There is a sufficient selection of low-cost, flavorful produce in markets to ensure varied salads at every meal. Most vegetable salads are based on one of the many green, leafy vegetables: lettuce such as romaine, iceberg, bibb, or Boston; chicory; watercress; endive; spinach; dandelion greens; escarole; or red, white, or Chinese cabbage.

Bibb lettuce is also known as limestone lettuce as it grows only in limestone soil. It has a small fragile head with leaves that shade from yellow to green. Reputed to be the finest lettuce in the world, it can be stored for only a few days.

Boston lettuce is available in a round, loosely-packed head. It has tender

salad greens
SHOPPER'S GUIDE

leaves and a mild, delicious flavor. Boston lettuce can be kept for only a day or two.

Bronze lettuce is garden lettuce with an appearance similar to leaf lettuce — big loose leaves without a head. The leaves are edged with bronze or red.

Cabbage comes in firmly-packed heads of thick, heavy leaves. These leaves may be either light green or purplish-red in color.

Chicory is a crisp vegetable with a slightly bitter taste. It has feathery leaves which spread out and are yellow at the center, deepening to green on the outside.

Dandelion greens have a tart flavor and dark green, long, thin leaves.

Endive has long, narrow, pale yellow heads with tightly-packed, arrow-like waxy leaves. It has a tangy flavor and can be kept a week or more.

Escarole features curly, firm, rough leaves with a bitter taste. It has a flat, spread-out head with a yellow center and dark green edges.

Field lettuce is soft and delightful in flavor. It is always a good buy and comes in small spears on delicate stems.

Iceberg lettuce, probably the most commonly used salad vegetable, has a round, firm head. This lettuce keeps very well and is crisp although not very flavorful.

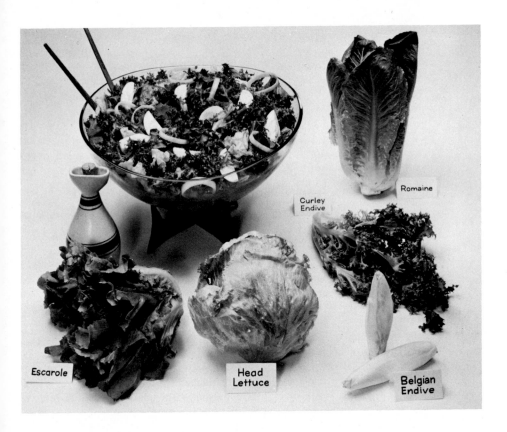

Romaine

Curley Endive

Escarole

Head Lettuce

Belgian Endive

Leaf or garden lettuce is tender, delicate, and very good-tasting. It has long, soft leaves with crumpled edges and does not keep well.

Spinach with its dark green leaves on stems is a long-time favorite salad vegetable. It is excellent for flavor and color contrast. For the best flavor, buy young spinach leaves only.

Watercress has a lively flavor. It comes in dark green petaled leaves on small stalks. It can be kept for several weeks in the refrigerator if you put the stems in a glass jar with a little water and cover the jar tightly.

Celery is a favorite vegetable frequently added to salads for flavor and texture contrast. Celery should have thick, clean stems and fresh-looking leaves. Avoid limp stalks and brownish leaves.

Chives, a member of the onion family often used in salads, should be bright green and in tufts when you purchase it. The best chives are those you grow yourself in a pot or small garden plot.

Beet tops are small in size and have a fresh flavor which contrasts nicely with lettuce. Only the tops from young beets should be used.

ASPARAGUS-RADISH SALAD

6 tbsp. olive oil	1 sm. clove of garlic, crushed
3 tbsp. vinegar	20 to 25 radishes, thinly sliced
1 tsp. salt	Cooked green asparagus, chilled
Pepper to taste	Salad greens

Mix the oil, vinegar, salt, pepper and garlic in a bowl. Add the radishes and marinate in refrigerator for 2 to 3 hours. Place the asparagus on salad greens. Drain the radishes and reserve marinade. Arrange the radishes on the asparagus and serve with reserved marinade. 4 servings.

Mrs. Aussie A. Miller, Newton, Texas

DELICIOUS GREEN ASPARAGUS SALAD

3 cans whole green asparagus	1 tsp. garlic salt
1 tsp. dried tarragon leaves	1 bottle Italian dressing
Pepper to taste	1/2 c. tarragon vinegar

Drain the asparagus well and place in layers in a shallow bowl, sprinkling each layer with tarragon leaves, pepper and garlic salt. Mix the salad dressing and vinegar and pour over asparagus. Marinate overnight at room temperature, then chill. Drain the asparagus and reserve marinade. Serve the asparagus on lettuce leaves and garnish with mayonnaise mixed with small amount of reserved marinade.

Mrs. Winthrop Rockefeller, Little Rock, Arkansas

AUTUMN GARDEN SALAD

3 c. shredded cabbage	1/2 c. sour cream
1 c. cherry tomato halves	1 tsp. curry powder
2 med. carrots, cut in strips	1/2 tsp. salt
1 sm. red onion, thinly sliced	4 slices drained fried bacon
1/4 c. sliced radishes	

Place the first 5 ingredients in a salad bowl and toss lightly. Combine the sour cream, curry powder and salt and pour over vegetables. Toss lightly. Crumble bacon over top and serve immediately. 6 servings.

Mrs. Hoyte Young, Portland, Tennessee

KIDNEY BEAN SALAD

1 15-oz. can red kidney beans	1/4 tsp. salt
1/2 c. diced celery	Dash of pepper
2 tbsp. chopped dill pickle	1 tbsp. salad oil
2 tbsp. minced onion	1 tbsp. mild vinegar

Drain the beans and place in a bowl. Add remaining ingredients and toss lightly. Chill. Garnish with onion rings or sliced hard-cooked eggs. 4-5 servings.

Blanford T. Anderson, Chatham, Virginia

SOUTHERN BEAN AND BACON SALAD

1 tsp. salt	3 tbsp. catsup
Dash of pepper	2 c. cooked green beans
1/2 tsp. sugar	Salad greens
1/3 c. salad oil	3 slices cooked bacon, crumbled
2 tbsp. vinegar	

Combine first 6 ingredients in a bowl and mix well. Add the beans and toss lightly. Place on salad greens and top with bacon. Garnish with radish roses. 6 servings. One can French-style green beans, drained, may be substituted for cooked beans.

Mrs. J. D. Williams, Florence, Alabama

CALYPSO SALAD

1 1-lb. can cut Blue Lake green beans	1/2 c. sliced onion rings
	1/4 c. basil wine vinegar
1 1-lb. 1-oz. can kidney beans	2 tbsp. salad oil
1 c. sliced celery	1/8 tsp. garlic powder
1/2 c. chopped green pepper	1/4 tsp. fines herbes
1/4 c. minced parsley	1/4 tsp. salt
1 qt. torn iceberg lettuce	Iceberg lettuce leaves

Drain the green beans and kidney beans and place in a bowl. Add the celery, green pepper, parsley, torn lettuce and onion rings and mix. Combine the vinegar, oil, garlic powder, fines herbes and salt in a jar and cover. Shake until well blended. Pour over bean mixture and toss lightly. Line a salad bowl with lettuce leaves and spoon bean mixture into lettuce. 6-8 servings.

Calypso Salad (above)

WALNUT ANTIPASTO SALAD

1 c. walnut halves or lge. pieces	1 6-oz. jar marinated artichoke
1 tbsp. salad oil	hearts
1/2 tsp. garlic salt	1/2 c. fresh brown mushrooms
1/4 tsp. mixed Italian herbs	2 pimentos
1 15-oz. can white kidney beans	1/2 c. pitted ripe olives
1 8 3/4-oz. can red kidney beans	6 sm. slices salami
1 8 3/4-oz. can garbanzos	1 1/2 qt. crisp mixed salad greens

Place the walnuts and oil in a skillet and stir over low heat for about 5 minutes or until lightly toasted. Sprinkle with garlic salt and Italian herbs and cool. Place all the beans in a large sieve, run under cold water and drain well. Drain the artichoke hearts and cut in halves. Slice the mushrooms. Cut the pimentos in quarters and drain the olives. Arrange the walnuts, beans, artichoke hearts, mushrooms, pimentos, olives and salami on lettuce in a chilled serving bowl and serve with Antipasto Dressing. 6 servings.

Antipasto Dressing

3/4 c. salad oil	1 tsp. seasoned salt
1/3 c. garlic-flavored red wine	1/2 tsp. seasoned pepper
vinegar	1/2 tsp. dry mustard
1 tbsp. honey	1 tbsp. grated Parmesan cheese
1/2 tsp. crumbled dried basil	

Place all ingredients in a jar and cover. Shake until well blended.

Photograph for this recipe on page 72

CABBAGE RELISH SALAD

3 c. shredded cabbage	3/4 tsp. salt
1/2 cucumber, diced	1/2 c. vinegar
1/3 c. diced celery	1/8 tsp. pepper
1/2 green pepper, diced	1/2 c. cream
1 tbsp. minced onion	

Crisp the cabbage, cucumber, celery and green pepper in iced water and drain well. Add remaining ingredients except cream and mix. Chill. Stir in the cream just before serving.

Mrs. O. J. Porter, Centertown, Kentucky

SKILLET SALAD

4 slices bacon	1 tbsp. finely chopped onion
1/4 c. vinegar	4 c. shredded cabbage
1 tbsp. brown sugar	1/2 c. chopped parsley
1 tsp. salt	

Cook the bacon in a skillet until crisp. Remove from skillet, drain and crumble. Add the vinegar, sugar, salt and onion to bacon fat in skillet and heat through. Remove from heat. Add the cabbage, parsley and bacon and toss lightly.

Mrs. Ernest Storek, Seymour, Texas

CREAM COLESLAW

4 c. shredded cabbage	3 tbsp. vinegar
1/2 c. minced celery	3 tbsp. sugar
1/4 c. minced green pepper	1 tsp. salt
2 tbsp. minced green onion	1/8 tsp. white pepper
1/4 c. minced sweet red pepper	1 tbsp. celery seed
3/4 c. sour cream	

Combine the cabbage, celery, green pepper, onion and red pepper. Combine remaining ingredients and pour over cabbage mixture. Mix lightly. Carrots may be substituted for red pepper. 6 servings.

Charlotte B. Love, Bells, Tennessee

CALIFORNIA CAESAR SALAD

1 c. peanut oil	1/2 tsp. salt
1 clove of garlic, crushed	1/4 tsp. dry mustard
2 c. bread cubes	1/4 tsp. pepper
2 heads romaine	1/3 c. lemon juice
1 head Boston lettuce	2 eggs, slightly beaten
1 bunch watercress	Dash of Worcestershire sauce
3/4 c. grated Parmesan cheese	1 2-oz. can anchovy fillets

Pour the peanut oil into a jar and add the garlic. Cover and let stand for at least 1 hour. Saute the bread cubes in 1/4 cup of the oil in a saucepan until golden brown. Tear the romaine, Boston lettuce and watercress into a large salad bowl and sprinkle with Parmesan cheese, salt, mustard and pepper. Pour remaining oil, lemon juice and eggs over salad. Add Worcestershire sauce, anchovy fillets and croutons and toss lightly until well mixed. 10-12 servings.

Photograph for this recipe on cover.

CAULIFLOWER SALAD

1 med. head cauliflower	1/2 tsp. salt
1/2 c. grated American cheese	1/2 c. French dressing

Wash the cauliflower thoroughly and break into flowerets. Slice each floweret 1/8 to 1/4 inch thick and place in a bowl. Sprinkle with grated cheese and salt and pour French dressing over all. Toss lightly. Serve on lettuce leaves, if desired. Cheddar cheese may be substituted for American cheese.

Mrs. Charles B. King, Decatur, Tennessee

Chick-Pea Salad (below)

CHICK-PEA SALAD

6 oz. Spanish or Italian sausage
1 1-lb. 4-oz. can chick-peas, drained
1 sm. onion, chopped
1/4 c. sliced sweet gherkins

1/4 c. sweet pickle liquid
1/2 tsp. salt
Dash of pepper
1 tbsp. wine vinegar
Pimento or red pepper strips

Cover the sausage with water in a skillet and bring to a boil. Reduce heat and simmer for 5 minutes. Drain. Slice the sausage and fry in same skillet until brown. Drain on paper towels. Combine the sausage, chick-peas, onion, gherkins, pickle liquid, salt, pepper and vinegar in a bowl and mix lightly. Chill. Garnish with pimento strips. 4 servings.

EL PIQUENO SALAD

1 12-oz. can Mexicorn
2 c. large curd cottage cheese
2 green onions with tops, minced
3/4 c. sour cream

1/2 c. salad mustard
Dash of hot sauce
3/4 c. crushed corn chips

Drain the corn and place in a bowl. Stir in the cottage cheese and onions and chill thoroughly. Combine remaining ingredients except corn chips and whip thoroughly. Add the corn chips to salad mixture. Pour the sour cream mixture over salad mixture and toss well. Serve on crisp lettuce leaves, if desired. 6-8 servings.

Mrs. Carl R. Payne, Denison, Texas

CORN SALAD

1 No. 2 can whole kernel corn
1 pimento, chopped
1 sm. onion, chopped
1 sm. green pepper, chopped

1 sm. cucumber, chopped
1/2 c. French dressing
Lettuce leaves

Drain the corn and place in a bowl. Add remaining ingredients except lettuce and mix well. Serve on lettuce. Mayonnaise may be substituted for French dressing. 4 servings.

Mrs. Judy Brumley, Kyle, Texas

STUFFED CUCUMBER SALAD

3 med. cucumbers
2 tomatoes
1/2 c. diced celery
1/2 tsp. salt

1/8 tsp. pepper
1 tbsp. chopped onion
Mayonnaise

Chill the cucumbers and tomatoes, Peel the cucumbers and cut in half lengthwise. Remove pulp from the centers, being careful not to break the outside. Drain the pulp and reserve. Peel the tomatoes, dice and drain well. Mix the reserved cucumber pulp, tomato, celery, salt, pepper and onion with enough mayonnaise to moisten. Fill cucumber halves with tomato mixture and chill. Serve on lettuce and garnish with green pepper rings, radishes or parsley.

Mrs. Woodrow Worrell, Hillsville, Virginia

SUPERB SOUR CREAM-CUCUMBERS

1/3 c. sour cream
1 tsp. finely minced onion
1 tsp. cider vinegar

1 lge. cucumber, thinly sliced
Salt to taste
1 tsp. dillseed

Place the sour cream, onion and vinegar in a mixing bowl and mix well. Season the cucumber with salt and dillseed, then add the sour cream mixture. Toss until cucumber is coated. Cover the bowl and refrigerate for 30 to 40 minutes. Serve on lettuce.

Mrs. Eulalie Woods, Gainesville, Texas

MUSTARD GREENS SALAD

2 c. finely chopped mustard
   greens
1 hard-boiled egg, chopped
1/2 tsp. salt

1/4 tsp. pepper
1/2 tsp. sugar
1 tbsp. mayonnaise
1 tsp. cider vinegar

Wash and drain the mustard greens. Mix all ingredients in a salad bowl and cover. Refrigerate for 15 minutes before serving.

Mrs. H. D. Nelms, Glenwood, Georgia

The Salad (below)

THE SALAD

2 c. sliced carrots	1/2 c. chopped Bermuda onion
1 10-oz. package frozen	2/3 c. sliced stuffed olives
green peas	1 lb. cooked bacon, crumbled
1 med. head iceberg lettuce,	Blender Mayonnaise
shredded	1 tsp. sugar
Salt and pepper to taste	Whole stuffed olives
1 c. sliced celery	Parsley

Cook the carrots in a small amount of boiling, salted water until crisp-tender. Drain and chill. Cook the peas according to package directions. Drain and chill. Place the lettuce in a large glass or other salad bowl and season with salt and pepper. Arrange the carrots, celery, peas, onion, sliced olives and bacon in layers over lettuce. Spread 1 cup Blender Mayonnaise over top and sprinkle with sugar. Garnish with whole olives and parsley and serve with remaining Blender Mayonnaise. Commercial mayonnaise may be substituted for Blender Mayonnaise. 8-10 servings.

Blender Mayonnaise

3 egg yolks	3/4 tsp. dry mustard
3 tbsp. wine vinegar	1 1/2 c. salad oil
1 1/2 tsp. salt	

Place the egg yolks, vinegar, salt, mustard and 1/2 cup oil in blender container and cover. Blend at high speed until just mixed, then turn blender off. Remove cover. Turn blender to low speed and add remaining oil in a steady stream. Blend until thoroughly combined. Chill until ready to use.

GALA GREENS

6 heads endive
1 bunch romaine
1 1-lb. jar sliced papaya

1 2-oz. can rolled fillets
of anchovies
French dressing

Chill the endive, romaine and papaya. Drain the papaya and anchovies. Arrange the endive, romaine and papaya in a salad bowl and add anchovies. Add enough French dressing to moisten and toss lightly. Garnish with croutons.

Naomi Bourne, House, New Mexico

GREEK SALAD PLATTER

1 med. cucumber
1 head Boston lettuce
2 carrots, coarsely grated
2 tomatoes, sliced
1/2 c. thinly sliced radishes

12 pitted ripe olives
1/2 tsp. dried oregano leaves
1/2 c. Italian-style salad
dressing

Peel and slice the cucumber. Line a salad bowl with outside leaves of lettuce. Break remaining lettuce into bite-sized pieces into bowl. Add the carrots, tomatoes, cucumber, radishes and olives and sprinkle with oregano. Pour dressing over all and toss until vegetables are coated. 6 servings.

Kathy Mashburn, Powhatan, Arkansas

HEALTH CLUB SALAD

1 c. diced celery
1 c. diced carrots
1/2 green pepper, diced

2 c. cottage cheese
1/2 c. Cheddar cheese dressing
2 c. shredded cabbage

Mix the celery, carrots, green pepper and cottage cheese with 1/4 cup Cheddar cheese dressing. Place the cabbage on individual salad plates and mound cottage cheese mixture on the cabbage. Serve with remaining cheese dressing.

Blanford T. Anderson, Chatham, Virginia

MARINATED OKRA SALAD

1 pkg. frozen whole okra
Juice of 1 lemon
1/2 c. salad oil

2 tbsp. horseradish
1/2 c. paper-thin onion slices
2 med. peeled sliced tomatoes

Prepare the okra according to package directions and drain. Combine the lemon juice, salad oil and horseradish. Place the okra, onion and tomato slices in a bowl and pour dressing over top. Marinate in refrigerator until chilled. Drain and serve.

Mrs. Reps O. Brown, Pegram, Tennessee

MUSHROOM RIO SALAD

1 lb. fresh mushrooms	1 hard-cooked egg, chopped
1 c. chopped celery	2 tbsp. minced green onion
2 pimentos, diced	Salt and pepper to taste
1 c. shredded lettuce	1 c. French dressing

Dice the mushrooms and place in a bowl. Add the celery, pimentos, lettuce, egg and onion. Season with salt and pepper and toss. Serve on crisp lettuce leaves with French dressing. 6 servings.

Mrs. S. B. Goodwin, Tombstone, Arizona

HOT GERMAN POTATO SALAD

6 slices bacon, chopped	1/4 c. water
1/4 c. chopped onion	3 tbsp. salad dressing
1 tbsp. flour	4 c. diced cooked potatoes
1 tbsp. sugar	2 hard-cooked eggs, sliced
1 tsp. salt	1 tbsp. minced parsley
Dash of pepper	1/2 tsp. celery seed
1/3 c. vinegar	

Cook the bacon in a skillet until crisp. Remove from skillet and drain. Drain off all except 2 tablespoons bacon drippings from skillet. Add the onion to skillet and cook until tender but not brown. Blend in the flour, sugar, salt and pepper. Add the vinegar and water and cook, stirring constantly, until thick. Remove from heat and stir in salad dressing and bacon. Pour over the potatoes and toss lightly. Place in a casserole. Bake in 350-degree oven for 20 minutes or until heated through. Top with eggs and sprinkle with parsley and celery seed. Serve hot. 8 servings.

Mrs. Ben T. Jacob, Georgetown, Texas

POTATO SALAD

5 lb. potatoes	1/2 c. chopped olives
1 env. onion salad dressing mix	1/2 c. chopped pickles
2 tsp. salt	4 hard-cooked eggs, chopped
2 c. chopped celery	1 c. mayonnaise
1/2 c. chopped green onions	1 tsp. celery seed (opt.)
1/2 c. chopped green pepper	

Cook the unpeeled potatoes in enough boiling water to cover until tender. Drain and cool slightly. Peel and slice thin. Place in a bowl. Prepare the salad dressing mix according to package directions, adding salt. Pour over warm potatoes and cool thoroughly. Add remaining ingredients and mix lightly. Chill. 20 servings.

MUSTARD-POTATO SALAD

6 med. potatoes, cooked in jackets	Salt and pepper to taste
1 c. diced celery	1/4 tsp. onion salt
1/2 c. chopped onion	1/8 tsp. celery salt
1/2 c. chopped sweet pickles	1 tbsp. prepared mustard
3 hard-cooked eggs, diced	1/2 c. sweet pickle vinegar
	1/2 c. mayonnaise

Peel and dice the potatoes and place in a bowl. Add remaining ingredients and mix well. Refrigerate overnight. Additional mayonnaise may be added just before serving if salad is too dry. 6 servings.

Mrs. C. Hallum, Burneyville, Oklahoma

GOURMET POTATO SALAD

1 c. creamed cottage cheese	1 c. diced green onions with tops
1 c. sour cream	1 c. diced celery
2 tsp. seasoned salt	1/2 c. diced green pepper
2 tsp. prepared mustard	3 hard-cooked eggs, chopped
4 c. diced cooked potatoes	1 1-oz. package bleu cheese

Combine the cottage cheese, sour cream, salt and mustard. Mix the potatoes, onions, celery, green pepper and eggs in a bowl. Add the sour cream mixture and mix gently. Chill for several hours to blend flavors. Crumble the bleu cheese and fold into salad just before serving. 6-8 servings.

Wanda Clement, Claudville, Virginia

Potato Salad (page 86)

FRESH SPINACH SALAD

1/2 lb. spinach	4 hard-cooked eggs, sliced
1 sm. Bermuda onion, sliced	French Dressing
1/4 c. diced celery	

Wash and dry the spinach and tear into bite-sized pieces. Place in a salad bowl. Add the onion, celery and eggs and toss lightly. Chill. Toss lightly with French Dressing just before serving. 8 servings.

French Dressing

1/4 c. olive oil	1 sm. clove of garlic, pressed
2 tbsp. wine	1/4 tsp. pepper
1 1/2 tsp. salt	1/4 tsp. monosodium glutamate

Combine all ingredients and mix well.

Wilma Mansel, West Columbia, Texas

SPRING SALAD

2 2/3 c. cottage cheese	1 c. chopped celery
1/2 c. skim milk	1 c. chopped radishes
2 tsp. lemon juice	1/2 c. chopped scallions or
3/4 tsp. salt	green onions
1 c. chopped green pepper	

Place first 4 ingredients in a blender container and blend until smooth. Mix remaining ingredients in a bowl. Pour the cottage cheese mixture over the celery mixture and toss lightly. 6 servings.

Mrs. P. R. Reese, Tucson, Arizona

STUFFED LETTUCE SALAD

1 lge. head lettuce	1 tbsp. minced pimento
1 3-oz. package cream cheese	1 tbsp. minced chives or onion
2 tbsp. crumbled bleu cheese	3 tbsp. mayonnaise
2 tbsp. grated carrot	Salt and pepper to taste
1 tbsp. minced green pepper	Paprika to taste
1/2 med. tomato, chopped	

Remove core from lettuce, then remove center leaves, leaving a shell. Combine remaining ingredients and blend thoroughly. Pack into lettuce shell and wrap in a damp cloth or plastic wrap. Chill for several hours. Slice crosswise and place on salad plates. Serve with mayonnaise or salad dressing. 6 servings.

Mrs. James Price, Alexandria, Virginia

TOSSED GREEN SALAD

1 sm. head lettuce	1 clove of garlic, halved
1/4 lb. spinach	2 scallions, minced
1/4 lb. curly endive	1/4 c. French dressing
1 bunch watercress	Salt and pepper to taste

Wash and drain the lettuce, spinach, endive and watercress and chill for 30 minutes. Wrap in a towel to dry. Rub a salad bowl with garlic. Tear or cut the greens into the salad bowl and add the scallions. Add French dressing and season with salt and pepper. Toss lightly until greens are coated with dressing. 4 servings.

Dianne Woods, Chatham, Virginia

GALEANO ARTICHOKE HEARTS

1 pkg. Italian salad dressing mix	1 c. boiling water
1 9-oz. package frozen artichoke hearts	2 tsp. vinegar
	1 tbsp. diced pimento
1 c. thinly sliced fresh mushrooms	1 c. mayonnaise or salad dressing
1 3-oz. package celery gelatin	

Prepare the salad dressing mix according to package directions. Cook the artichokes according to package directions. Drain, cool and cut into halves. Marinate the artichokes and mushrooms in dressing for 1 hour. Drain, reserving dressing. Refrigerate dressing. Dissolve the gelatin in boiling water in a bowl. Add vinegar and 7 ice cubes and stir until slightly thickened. Add the artichokes, mushrooms and pimento and mix well. Turn into a 1-quart mold and chill overnight. Beat mayonnaise with reserved dressing until smooth. Unmold salad on serving plate and serve with mayonnaise mixture. 4-6 servings.

Mrs. F. G. Young, Memphis, Tennessee

WATERCRESS A LA DENNIS

2 eggs, beaten	1/3 c. vinegar
2 c. salad oil	2 tbsp. paprika
2 tbsp. horseradish	Dash of pepper
1/4 c. catsup	1 tbsp. Worcestershire sauce
1/4 lge. onion, grated	Sliced bacon
1 tbsp. salt	Watercress

Place all ingredients except bacon and watercress in a blender container and blend until mixed. Place 1 slice bacon for each serving in a frypan and cook until crisp. Drain, then crumble. Toss desired amount of watercress with bacon in a salad bowl and serve with dressing.

Mrs. J. D. Wigley, Huntsville, Alabama

Fresh Watercress Salad (below)

FRESH WATERCRESS SALAD

2 bunches fresh watercress
3 stalks fresh celery, sliced
3 fresh tomatoes, cut in wedges
1 c. pitted ripe olives
Salt and pepper to taste

Juice of 1/2 lemon
1/4 c. salad oil
2 tbsp. vinegar
1/4 clove of garlic, crushed

Tear the watercress into bite-sized pieces and place in a salad bowl. Add the celery, tomatoes and olives and mix. Sprinkle with salt and pepper. Place the lemon juice, oil, vinegar and garlic in a jar and cover. Shake well. Pour over salad and toss lightly.

TOMATO-ANCHOVY SALAD

2 lge. tomatoes
Lettuce or watercress
1 sm. onion, sliced thin
6 rolled anchovies

1 tsp. lemon juice
1 hard-cooked egg yolk
French dressing

Peel the tomatoes and cut each tomato into 3 slices. Chill. Arrange lettuce on 6 salad plates and place tomato slice on each. Cover with onion slices and top each serving with an anchovy. Sprinkle with lemon juice. Sieve the egg yolk and sprinkle on each serving. Serve with French dressing. 6 servings.

Mrs. Q. A. Bradley, Taft, Texas

STUFFED TOMATO SALAD

4 med. tomatoes
1 1/2 c. cottage cheese

2 tsp. minced onion
1 tbsp. chopped parsley

2 tbsp. chopped pimento   **Low-calorie dressing**
Lettuce

Wash and peel the tomatoes and cut out stems. Remove pulp from centers. Mix the cottage cheese, onion, parsley and pimento in a mixing bowl thoroughly and fill centers of tomatoes with cottage cheese mixture. Chill. Place tomatoes on lettuce and serve with the dressing. 4 servings.

Mrs. J. D. Long, Mesa, Arizona

ASPARAGUS MOLD

1 env. unflavored gelatin	1/2 c. heavy cream, whipped
1/4 c. cold water	1 tsp. salt
1 1-lb. can asparagus	2 tbsp. lemon juice
1/2 c. mayonnaise	1 c. blanched slivered almonds

Soften the gelatin in water in a bowl. Drain the asparagus and reserve liquid. Add enough water to reserved liquid to make 1 cup liquid and pour into a saucepan. Bring to a boil. Add the gelatin and stir until dissolved. Chill until partially set. Fold in the mayonnaise, whipped cream, salt, lemon juice, asparagus and almonds and place in a mold. Chill until set. Serve with additional mayonnaise.

Mrs. L. M. DeShong, Paris, Texas

COTTAGE CHEESE-ASPARAGUS MOUSSE

2 9-oz. packages frozen asparagus	2 tbsp. lemon juice
1 tbsp. unflavored gelatin	1/2 tsp. prepared mustard
1 1/2 c. cottage cheese	1/2 tsp. salt
	1 c. blanched slivered almonds

Cook the asparagus according to package directions. Drain and reserve liquid. Soften the gelatin in 1/4 cup water. Add enough water to reserved asparagus liquid to make 1 cup liquid and heat to boiling point. Stir in gelatin until dissolved. Chill until thickened. Sieve the cottage cheese or blend in a blender until smooth and creamy and stir in the lemon juice, mustard and salt. Chop the asparagus and fold in gelatin. Fold in the cottage cheese mixture and almonds and turn into a 1-quart mold. Chill until firm. Unmold on salad greens.

Alberta Cramer, Townville, South Carolina

GREEN ONION SALAD

1 3-oz. package lemon gelatin	1 c. chopped celery
1 c. hot water	4 sm. green onions, chopped
1 c. cottage cheese	2/3 c. salad dressing

Dissolve the gelatin in hot water in a bowl and cool. Stir in remaining ingredients and pour into a 9 x 9-inch dish. Chill until firm. Cut in squares and serve on lettuce leaves. 6 servings.

Mrs. R. G. Gipson, Perkinston, Mississippi

MOLDED VEGETABLE SALAD

1 3-oz. package celery gelatin	1/4 c. finely chopped green
1 c. hot water	pepper
1/4 c. cold water	1 tbsp. grated onion
1 1/2 tsp. vinegar	1/4 tsp. seasoned salt
1 c. diced red beets, drained	1/2 c. evaporated milk
1/2 c. thinly sliced celery	1 tbsp. lemon juice

Dissolve the gelatin in hot water in a bowl. Add the cold water, vinegar, beets, celery, green pepper, onion and seasoned salt and mix well. Chill until slightly thickened. Pour undiluted milk into a refrigerator tray and freeze until ice crystals form around edge of tray. Whip until stiff. Add the lemon juice and whip until very stiff. Fold into gelatin mixture and pour into a 5-cup mold. Chill until firm.

Mrs. Joe Wiles, Moreland, Georgia

SURPRISE BROCCOLI MOLD

2 pkg. frozen broccoli	1 c. mayonnaise
1 env. unflavored gelatin	Salt and pepper to taste
1 can consomme	Sliced avocado (opt.)
1/2 sm. onion, grated	Olives (opt.)
2 hard-cooked eggs, diced	Shrimp (opt.)
1 tbsp. lemon juice	

Cook the broccoli in 2 1/2 cups boiling, salted water until well done. Drain and mash or blend until smooth. Soften the gelatin in 1/2 cup cold water. Pour the consomme into a saucepan and bring to a boil. Stir in the gelatin until dissolved. Add broccoli and cool. Add the onion, eggs, lemon juice, mayonnaise, salt and pepper and pour into a ring mold. Refrigerate until firm. Unmold onto serving dish and place avocado, olives and shrimp in center of mold. 6-8 servings.

Mrs. R. D. Gregory, Baton Rouge, Louisiana

ALFRESCO OLIVE SALAD

1 qt. diced carrots	1/4 c. chopped green onions
1 pt. diced potatoes	1 sm. clove of garlic, minced
1 1/2 c. canned pitted ripe	1 tbsp. butter
olives	1/2 c. California Dressing

Cook the carrots and potatoes in boiling, salted water for about 7 minutes or until just tender. Do not overcook. Drain and cool. Cut the olives into quarters. Cook the onions and garlic in butter in a saucepan until soft but not browned. Combine the carrot mixture, olives and onion mixture with California Dressing and mix lightly. Spoon into an oiled 6-cup mold and press down lightly. Cover and refrigerate overnight. Unmold and garnish with ripe olives, carrot curls and watercress. 6-8 servings.

California Dressing

2/3 c. salad oil
1/3 c. garlic wine vinegar
1 1/2 tsp. seasoned salt
1/4 tsp. seasoned pepper

1/2 tsp. paprika
1/2 tsp. sugar
2 tbsp. crumbled blue cheese
2 canned pimentos, mashed

Combine first 6 ingredients and add the cheese and pimentos. Beat well or whip in blender. 1 1/2 cups.

ICEBERG BORSCHT SALAD

1 lge. head western iceberg
   lettuce
3 env. unflavored gelatin
2 c. water
1 tbsp. sugar
Salt
2 1-lb. cans sliced pickled beets

1/4 c. frozen orange juice
   concentrate
1/4 c. sliced green onion
1 pt. sour cream
1/4 c. prepared horseradish
Pepper to taste

Core, rinse and drain the lettuce. Place in a plastic bag or plastic wrap and chill. Soften the gelatin in water in a small saucepan, then heat until gelatin is completely dissolved. Remove from heat and stir in the sugar and 1/2 teaspoon salt. Drain the beets and reserve liquid. Stir reserved liquid into gelatin mixture. Stir in the orange juice concentrate and chill until partially set. Cut beets into strips and fold into gelatin mixture. Turn into a 6 1/2-cup ring mold and chill until firm. Cut the lettuce into bite-sized chunks. Unmold salad on a serving plate. Fill center with lettuce and sprinkle with onion. Mix sour cream with horseradish, salt to taste and pepper and serve with salad. 10-12 servings.

Iceberg Borscht Salad (above)

93

Vegetable Salad Ring (below)

VEGETABLE SALAD RING

1 env. unflavored gelatin	1/4 c. mayonnaise or salad
1/4 c. lemon juice	dressing
1 can cream of chicken soup	2 tbsp. chopped green pepper
1/2 c. chopped celery	2 tbsp. sliced stuffed olives

Soften the gelatin in lemon juice. Heat 1/4 can soup in a saucepan over low heat. Add the gelatin and stir until dissolved. Add remaining soup and chill until slightly thickened. Stir in remaining ingredients. Rinse a 1-quart mold with cold water and pour salad mixture into mold. Chill until firm. Unmold and serve on crisp greens. 6 servings.

ELEGANT PEA SALAD

1 3-oz. package lemon gelatin	1 tsp. grated onion
1/2 tsp. salt	1 tbsp. horseradish
1 c. hot water	1/2 c. chopped celery
1/2 c. cold water	1 No. 2 can peas, drained
1 tbsp. vinegar	1 No. 2 can julienne beets

Dissolve the gelatin and salt in hot water in a bowl and stir in the cold water, vinegar, onion and horseradish. Chill until slightly thickened and add the celery. Divide into 2 equal parts. Add peas to 1 part and fill individual molds 1/2 full. Chill until almost firm. Drain the beets and add to remaining gelatin mixture. Spoon over congealed layers and chill until firm. 4-6 servings.

Mrs. L. D. Grimes, Maud, Texas

CREME DE CUCUMBER SALAD

2 c. boiling water	1 c. grated cucumbers
1 6-oz. package lime gelatin	1 tbsp. grated onion
1 tbsp. vinegar	1 tbsp. horseradish
1 c. mayonnaise	

Pour the boiling water over gelatin in a bowl and stir until dissolved. Add the vinegar and mayonnaise and chill until partially set. Whip until fluffy. Add remaining ingredients and place in mold. Chill until firm.

Mrs. R. W. Thomas, Thomasville, Georgia

PIQUANT SALAD

2 tbsp. unflavored gelatin	1 tsp. salt
1/2 c. cold water	1/8 tsp. hot sauce
2 c. boiling water	1 1/2 c. shredded cabbage
1/2 c. cider vinegar	1 c. diced celery
2 tbsp. lemon juice	1/4 c. chopped pimento
2 tsp. Worcestershire sauce	1 c. tiny green peas
1/2 c. sugar	1 c. cut green beans

Soften the gelatin in cold water in a bowl for 5 minutes. Add the boiling water and stir until dissolved. Stir in the vinegar, lemon juice, Worcestershire sauce, sugar, salt and hot sauce and chill until partially set. Stir in remaining ingredients and turn into a mold. Chill until firm. 10-12 servings.

Mrs. Henry Sherrer, Bay City, Texas

SOUFFLE POTATO SALAD

2 c. diced cooked potatoes	1 3-oz. package lemon gelatin
5 tbsp. vinegar	1 c. hot water
1/3 c. chopped dill pickles	1/2 c. cold water
1 tsp. salt	1/2 c. mayonnaise
1/8 tsp. pepper	1 tsp. prepared mustard
1/2 tsp. dried dill	2 hard-cooked eggs, sliced
2 tbsp. sliced green onion	

Combine the potatoes with 2 tablespoons vinegar, dill pickles, salt, pepper, dill and green onion. Dissolve the gelatin in hot water in a bowl. Add the cold water, remaining vinegar, mayonnaise and mustard and beat with rotary beater until smooth. Pour into refrigerator tray and place in freezing unit until mixture is firm 1 inch from edge. Turn into a bowl and beat with rotary beater or electric mixer until fluffy. Fold in the potato mixture and eggs. Pour into 1-quart ring mold and chill until firm. Unmold and serve on salad greens. 6 servings.

Mrs. E. D. Volmar, Beaumont, Texas

SPINACH-COTTAGE CHEESE SALAD

1 3-oz. package lemon gelatin
1 c. hot water
1/2 c. cold water
1 1/2 tsp. vinegar
1/2 c. mayonnaise

Salt and pepper to taste
1 c. chopped spinach
3/4 c. cottage cheese
1/3 c. diced celery
1 tbsp. finely chopped onion

Dissolve the gelatin in hot water in a bowl. Add cold water, vinegar, mayonnaise, salt and pepper and blend well with a rotary beater. Pour into refrigerator tray. Place in freezing unit for 15 to 20 minutes or until firm 1 inch from edge of tray. Place in a bowl and whip with rotary beater until fluffy. Fold in the spinach, cottage cheese, celery and onion and pour into a mold. Chill until firm.

Mrs. Ernest Stouk, Seymour, Texas

SPINACH SALAD MOLD

2 pkg. frozen chopped spinach
2 pkg. unflavored gelatin
1 can consomme
4 hard-cooked eggs, diced
3/4 c. mayonnaise

1 3/4 tsp. salt
2 tbsp. lemon juice
2 tbsp. Worcestershire sauce
Dash of hot sauce

Cook the spinach according to package directions and drain. Cool. Soften the gelatin in 1/2 cup cold consomme. Heat remaining consomme in a saucepan. Add the gelatin and stir until dissolved. Chill until partially set. Add the eggs, mayonnaise and remaining ingredients and mix well. Fold in the spinach and place in a 13 x 9 x 2-inch pan. Chill until set. Cut in squares to serve.

Mrs. T. S. Fulton, Panama City, Florida

TOMATO ASPIC WITH ONION-SOUR CREAM DRESSING

1 No. 2 can tomatoes
1 tbsp. unflavored gelatin
1/2 c. cold water
1 tsp. grated onion

1/2 tsp. salt
1/4 tsp. celery salt
1 tsp. sugar
2 tbsp. vinegar

Place the tomatoes in a saucepan and bring to a boil. Press through a sieve. Soften the gelatin in cold water and dissolve in hot tomato puree. Add remaining ingredients and pour into 6 individual molds. Chill until set. Two cups tomato juice may be substituted for tomatoes and water.

Onion-Sour Cream Dressing

1 tbsp. mayonnaise
1/4 c. chopped onion
1 c. sour cream

1/4 tsp. chopped parsley
Salt to taste

Combine all ingredients in a bowl and serve with salad.

Mrs. J. B. Roberts, Perry, Florida

HORSERADISH-TOMATO ASPIC

1 3-oz. package lemon gelatin	2 tsp. grated onion
1 c. hot tomato juice	1 1/2 tsp. salt
2 tsp. prepared horseradish	Dash of cayenne
1 c. cold tomato juice	

Dissolve the gelatin in hot tomato juice in a bowl. Stir in remaining ingredients and pour into a mold. Chill until firm. 4-6 servings.

Chili-Cream Dressing

1/2 c. mayonnaise	1/4 c. chili sauce
1/2 c. sour cream	

Combine all ingredients in a bowl and chill. Serve over salad.

Mrs. B. C. Goins, Chattanooga, Tennessee

VEGETABLE PLATTER

English peas	Cooked asparagus
Sliced cucumber	Pimento-stuffed green olives
Sliced string beans	Oil and vinegar dressing
Sliced California avocado	

Place the peas, cucumber, beans, avocado, asparagus and olives on a serving platter. Serve with the oil and vinegar dressing.

Vegetable Platter (above)

fruit salads

Low in calories, high in flavor appeal, fruit salads are favorites with everyone. *Southern Living* homemakers serve them to transform an ordinary casserole supper into an extraordinary meal . . . to highlight the flavor of a great beef or pork roast . . . to introduce a cool and light note into a heavily spiced dinner . . . or as the main course for ladies' luncheons and summer suppers.

The abundant varieties of fresh, canned, and frozen fruit invite homemakers to develop an endless range of fruit salad recipes. Southern women have responded to this invitation by creating eye-appealing, mouth-watering, and nutritious fruit salads for every occasion. The very best of these recipes are included in the pages that follow.

Here you'll find Snowball Salad — a bright dish based on that favorite southern fruit, peaches . . . Fresh Pear and Roquefort Salad — a lively taste treat certain to sparkle up any meal . . . Molded Cottage Cheese and Pineapple Salad — just right to highlight your supper . . . and many other home-tested recipes.

These and all the recipes in this section are the favorites of the women who submitted them to be part of the Southern Living Cookbook Library. They are the dishes for which these women have earned their reputations as unusually good cooks. And they are yours in this chapter featuring the wonderful variety of fruit salads.

In buying any fruit — fresh, canned, or frozen — let your choice of salads dictate the grade and physical appearance of the fruit you purchase. Fruit for a display salad — one that doubles as the center of attraction — should be top quality in appearance as well as taste. But fruit which is going to be mixed with salad vegetables or meat does not have to be of perfect appearance . . . especially if you are going to dice or chop it before it goes into the salad! When buying fresh fruit, look for color and firmness as guides to quality. Most ripe fruit will yield to gentle pressure. If it is either very soft or does not yield, don't buy it.

The chart below gives the calorie value of fresh, frozen, and canned fruit which is often used to prepare salads. Also included are calorie values of nuts often found in fruit salads.

general directions

FRUIT AND NUT CALORIE CHART		
FRUIT OR NUT	**AMOUNT**	**CALORIES**
APPLES:		
cubed or sliced	1 cup	85
raw	1 medium (2½" diameter)	70
APRICOTS:		
canned, syrup pack	1 cup	220
canned, water pack	1 cup	90
dried	three	55
AVOCADOS	1/2 peeled	185
BANANAS	1 medium (6" x 1½")	85
BLACKBERRIES:		
canned, syrup pack	1 cup	216
canned, water pack	1 cup	105
raw	1 cup	85
BLUEBERRIES:		
canned, syrup pack	1 cup	245
canned, water pack	1 cup	90
frozen, without sugar	3 ounces	52
raw	1 cup	85
BRAZIL NUTS:		
shelled	1 cup	905
	one	28
CANTALOUPES:		
1/2 melon	5" diameter	40
	1 cup diced	30
CASHEW NUTS		
	one	20
	7 ounces	165
	1 cup	770
CHERRIES:		
pitted	1 cup	65
red sour, canned	1 cup	110
COCONUT:		
dried	1 cup	360
fresh, shredded	1 cup	320
DATES, pitted	1 cup	505

FRUIT AND NUT CALORIE CHART

FRUIT OR NUT	AMOUNT	CALORIES
FIGS:		
canned, syrup pack	1/2 cup	110
dried	1 large (2" x 1")	60
FILBERT NUTS	six	50
FRUIT COCKTAIL	1 cup	195
GOOSEBERRIES, raw	1 cup	59
GRAPEFRUIT:		
canned, syrup pack	1 cup	170
raw, sections	1 cup	75
raw	1/2 medium	50
GRAPES, raw:		
Concord	1 cup	70
Tokay, Thompson	1 cup	100
ORANGES:		
sections	1 cup	85
	1 medium (3" diameter)	70
PEACHES:		
canned, syrup pack	1 cup	200
canned, water pack	1 cup	75
dried, cooked without sugar	1 cup	220
frozen	1/2 cup	105
raw, sliced	1 cup	65
raw, whole	1 medium	35
PEANUTS, shelled	1 cup halves	805
	10 kernels	55
PEARS:		
canned, syrup pack	1 cup	195
canned, water pack	1 cup	80
raw	one	100
PECANS:		
halves	1 cup	740
halves	one	10
chopped	1 tbsp.	50
PINEAPPLE:		
canned, syrup pack	1 cup crushed	205
	2 small slices	95
frozen	4 ounces	95
raw, diced	1 cup	75
raw, sliced	3/4" x 3 1/2"	45
PLUMS, raw	one, 2½" diameter	30
PRUNES:		
dried, cooked without sugar	1 cup	305
dried, cooked with sugar	1 cup	520
uncooked	4 medium	70
RAISINS, dried	1 cup	460
	1 tbsp.	29
RASPBERRIES:		
black, raw	1 cup	80
frozen	1/2 cup	120
red, raw	1 cup	70
STRAWBERRIES:		
fresh	1 cup	55
frozen	1/2 cup	120
TANGERINES	1 medium (2½" diameter)	40
WALNUT HALVES		
	1 cup	650
	one	10
	1 tbsp., chopped	50
WATERMELONS	1 wedge (4" x 8")	120

CINNAMON-APPLE SALAD

1 1/2 c. water	1/4 c. chopped nuts
1/2 c. sugar	Salt to taste
1/2 c. red cinnamon candies	Mayonnaise
6 peeled apples, cored	Lettuce
1 8-oz. package cream cheese	

Combine the water, sugar, and cinnamon candies in a saucepan and heat until cinnamon candies are dissolved. Place the apples in syrup and simmer, turning frequently, until apples are tender. Drain and chill. Combine the cream cheese, nuts and salt with enough mayonnaise to moisten. Stuff the apples with cheese mixture and serve on lettuce leaf.

Mrs. R. C. Bishop, Birmingham, Alabama

HOT APPLE SALAD

4 or 5 apples, diced	1/2 tsp. dry mustard
1/2 c. raisins	2 c. milk
1/2 c. flaked coconut	1 egg, slightly beaten
1 c. sugar	2 tbsp. butter
1 tbsp. flour	Juice of 1 lemon
Dash of salt	3/4 c. chopped nuts (opt.)

Combine the apples, raisins and coconut in a large bowl. Place the sugar, flour, salt and mustard in a saucepan. Stir in the milk and egg and cook until thickened, stirring frequently. Add butter and lemon juice and mix well. Pour over the apple mixture while hot and mix. Add nuts and mix well. 6-8 servings.

Mrs. E. W. Alexander, Galveston, Texas

STUFFED APPLES

1 c. sugar	Juice of 1 lemon
1 1/2 c. water	Red food coloring
Grated rind of 1 lemon	6 pared apples, cored

Mix the sugar, water, lemon rind and juice and enough food coloring for desired shade in a saucepan and bring to a boil. Add the apples and simmer until tender. Cool apples in the syrup. Drain apples.

Dressing

2 tsp. flour	1 tbsp. vinegar
1/4 c. sugar	Juice of 1 lemon
1/4 tsp. salt	1 egg, well beaten

1/2 c. cream cheese
1 c. whipping cream, whipped
1 c. diced pineapple

1/2 c. chopped celery
1/2 c. chopped pecans

Mix first 3 ingredients in a saucepan. Add the vinegar and lemon juice and mix. Cook over low heat until thickened, stirring frequently. Stir in the egg quickly and cook for several minutes. Cool, then beat in the cream cheese. Fold in the whipped cream, pineapple, celery and pecans and stuff in apples. Serve on lettuce leaves with remaining Dressing.

Mrs. J. A. Satterfield, Fort Worth, Texas

RED DELICIOUS CABBAGE SLAW

1/4 c. honey
2 tbsp. wine vinegar
1 tsp. horseradish
1/2 tsp. salt
1   8 1/2-oz. can crushed
     pineapple
1 med. head white cabbage

3 red Delicious apples
1 c. seeded Tokay grapes,
    halved
1/2 c. chopped cashew nuts
    or almonds
2 tbsp. lemon juice
1/2 c. water

Mix first 5 ingredients in a jar and cover. Chill. Wash the cabbage and remove and reserve 4 or 5 outer leaves. Place in refrigerator to crisp. Shred remaining cabbage fine. Core and dice 2 unpared apples directly into the cabbage. Add 1/2 cup grapes and the cashew nuts and toss. Shake the pineapple dressing and stir into apple mixture. Line a serving dish or salad bowl with reserved cabbage leaves and fill with salad mixture. Core and slice remaining unpared apple into 9 or 10 slices and dip into mixture of lemon juice and water. Place remaining grapes in center of salad and arrange apple slices around 1 end and down the sides to resemble a cluster of grapes and leaves. 6-8 generous servings.

Red Delicious Cabbage Slaw (above)

WALDORF SPIRAL SALAD

1/3 c. lemon juice	1 c. miniature marshmallows
4 c. cold water	1/4 c. mayonnaise
6 red apples	1/4 c. whipped cream
1 c. diced celery	1/2 c. coarsely chopped walnuts
1/3 c. seedless raisins	6 lettuce cups

Mix 3 tablespoons lemon juice and the water in a bowl. Cut the peelings from apples thickly in spiral fashion, being sure each peeling is long and unbroken. Place peelings in the lemon water to keep color bright. Core the apples and dice fine. Sprinkle with remaining lemon juice. Combine diced apple, celery, raisins, marshmallows and mayonnaise in a bowl and fold in the whipped cream and walnuts. Curl each peeling into cup shape and place on a lettuce leaf. Fill with salad.

Mrs. Shirley Boddie, Calvin, Louisiana

AVOCADO DELIGHT

2 avocados	Salad greens
Lemon juice	Salad dressing
24 fresh melon balls	

Cut avocados lengthwise and remove seeds. Brush lightly with lemon juice. Fill each avocado half with 6 melon balls and arrange on salad plate. Garnish with greens and serve with salad dressing. One 1-pound package frozen melon balls, thawed, may be substituted for fresh melon balls. 4 servings.

June Lunsford, Mena, Arkansas

BALTIMORE SALAD

3 peeled avocados, halved	3 peeled grapefruit, sectioned
1/2 pt. cottage cheese	Strawberries
Leaf lettuce	French dressing
4 lge. peeled oranges, sectioned	

Fill each half of avocado with cottage cheese and invert on lettuce leaf. Place alternate sections of orange and grapefruit around each avocado piece to resemble flower petals and place a strawberry between each orange and grapefruit section. Serve with French dressing. 6 servings.

Mrs. Ruth Phillips, Mt. Pleasant, South Carolina

ORANGE AND AVOCADO SALAD

2 avocados	1/4 c. fresh orange juice
3 fresh oranges	1/2 tsp. paprika
3/4 c. salad dressing or	1/2 tsp. salt
mayonnaise	Iceberg lettuce

Peel, seed and slice the avocados. Peel, seed and slice the oranges. Mix the salad dressing, orange juice, paprika and salt well. Place alternate slices of avocado and orange on lettuce leaves and drizzle with dressing. 6 servings.

Photograph for this recipe on page 2.

GOLDEN SUNBURST APPLE SALAD

3 golden Delicious apples	1 c. seedless grapes
1 pink grapefruit	Lettuce or spinach leaves
1 pkg. frozen melon balls	Lemon juice (opt.)

Core and slice the apples. Peel and section the grapefruit. Thaw and drain the melon balls. Arrange fruits decoratively in a salad bowl or tray lined with lettuce. Sprinkle apple slices with lemon juice diluted with water if salad is not to be served immediately. One cup fresh melon balls may be substituted for frozen melon balls. 4-6 servings.

Cardamom Salad Dressing

1/2 c. salad oil	1/2 tsp. salt
1/2 c. evaporated milk	1 tsp. sugar
1/4 c. lemon juice	1/4 tsp. ground cardamom

Place all ingredients in electric blender container and cover. Blend for a several seconds or until smooth and thickened. Chill. Serve on salad. Ingredients may be placed in a pint jar, covered tightly and shaken vigorously until creamy and smoothly blended.

Golden Sunburst Apple Salad (above)

BANANA-PEANUT SALAD

1 egg, beaten	1 tbsp. sugar
1/2 c. vinegar	Bananas
1/2 c. water	Chopped salted peanuts

Combine the egg, vinegar, water and sugar in a saucepan and bring to a boil, stirring constantly. Cool. Peel the bananas and cut in thick slices. Dip in dressing and roll in peanuts. Serve on crisp lettuce leaves.

Mrs. Fran La Duke, Louisville, Kentucky

STUFFED BANANA SALAD

1/4 c. peanut butter	Mayonnaise
2 tbsp. chopped raisins	Lemon juice
4 sm. bananas	Chopped salted peanuts

Mix the peanut butter with raisins. Peel and split bananas lengthwise and fill sandwich-fashion with peanut butter mixture. Roll in mayonnaise thinned with lemon juice, then in peanuts. Serve on lettuce and garnish with red cherry or strawberry.

Mrs. F. D. Canaday, Walterboro, South Carolina

BRAZILIAN FRUIT SALAD

1 red apple	2 tbsp. sliced Brazil nuts
1/2 c. red grapes	1/4 tsp. dried mint leaves (opt.)
1 11-oz. can mandarin oranges, drained	1 tsp. lemon juice
1 banana, sliced	3 tbsp. mayonnaise or salad dressing
1/4 c. maraschino cherries	2 tbsp. sour cream
1 c. coarsely chopped celery	Salad greens

Core and slice the apple. Halve and seed the grapes. Combine the oranges, banana, apple, cherries, grapes, celery and nuts in a bowl. Add the mint leaves and sprinkle with lemon juice. Blend the mayonnaise with sour cream and combine with fruit mixture. Serve on salad greens. 4-6 servings.

Cindy Mann, Lexington, Mississippi

CHERRY AND BLACKBERRY SALAD

2 c. large cherries	Lettuce
2 c. blackberries	1 c. chopped nuts
1 c. chopped celery	Mayonnaise

Wash the cherries and blackberries and drain well. Arrange the cherries, blackberries and celery on lettuce and sprinkle with nuts. Serve with mayonnaise.

Mrs. Wilbur Jenkins, Sadieville, Kentucky

CANTALOUPE FRUIT SALAD

1 med. cantaloupe, peeled	1 c. strawberries
Lettuce	1 lge. bunch white grapes
3 peeled oranges, sliced	1 c. yogurt
3 peeled peaches, sliced	1/2 c. mayonnaise
2 peeled nectarines, sliced	1/2 c. bleu cheese dressing
Pineapple slices	

Cut ends from cantaloupe and reserve. Slice center of cantaloupe crosswise into 5 rings. Shape balls from reserved cantaloupe with melon ball scoop. Place cantaloupe rings on lettuce. Arrange orange, peach, nectarine and pineapple slices in center and on top of cantaloupe rings and add strawberries and cantaloupe balls. Place a small cluster of grapes by each ring. Combine remaining ingredients and mix well. Serve with salad. 5 servings.

Helen Sergent, Gate City, Virginia

LOW-CALORIE LUNCH

2 lb. cottage cheese	2 tbsp. chopped green pepper
2 tbsp. chopped onion	2 tbsp. chopped celery
2 tbsp. chopped carrot	Fresh blueberries

Mix the cottage cheese, onion, carrot, green pepper and celery and place on a serving dish. Rinse and drain the blueberries and place around cottage cheese mixture. Calorie count is 71 for each 1/3 cup cottage cheese and 42 for each 1/2 cup blueberries.

Low-Calorie Lunch (above)

BEST CRANBERRY SALAD

4 c. fresh cranberries	2 c. halved red grapes, seeded
2 c. sugar	1/2 c. chopped walnuts
1 can pineapple tidbits	1 c. heavy cream, whipped

Grind the cranberries coarsely and mix with sugar. Refrigerate overnight. Drain the pineapple and cranberries well. Mix the pineapple, cranberries, grapes and walnuts and fold in the whipped cream. Serve on lettuce, if desired. 6 servings.

Mrs. J. W. Hopkins, Abilene, Texas

CRANBERRY-PINEAPPLE SALAD

1 can cranberry sauce	1 carton cottage cheese
1 can sliced pineapple	6 maraschino cherries
Lettuce	

Chill the cranberry sauce. Drain the pineapple. Cut the cranberry sauce into slices and place on lettuce cups. Place 1 slice pineapple over each slice of cranberry sauce. Place 1 rounded tablespoon cottage cheese in center of the pineapple and place a cherry on top.

Mrs. Janice P. Cabler, Nashville, Tennessee

CRANBERRY SALAD

3 c. fresh cranberries	1 pkg. miniature marshmallows
1 1/2 c. sugar	1 c. chopped nuts
1 No. 2 can crushed pineapple, chilled	1/2 pt. heavy cream, whipped

Grind the cranberries and place in a bowl. Stir in the sugar and cover. Chill overnight. Add the pineapple, marshmallows and nuts. Fold in the whipped cream and chill. May be refrigerated, covered, for several days.

Mrs. Noah McFodden, Paris, Texas

FAR EAST FRUIT SALAD

2 c. grapefruit sections	1 c. canned mandarin orange
1 1/2 c. pineapple chunks	sections, drained
1 5-oz. can water chestnuts	1/4 c. French dressing
1 5-oz. can chow mein noodles	

Drain the grapefruit sections and pineapple chunks. Drain and slice the water chestnuts. Place the chow mein noodles on 6 individual salad plates. Arrange the orange sections, grapefruit sections, pineapple chunks and water chestnuts on noodles and top with French dressing.

Ann Kirby, San Augustine, Texas

PEACH SYMPHONY SALAD

1 1-lb. 13-oz. can cling peach halves	Lettuce
1 lge. grapefruit	1 c. fresh strawberries
1 banana	Salad dressing
Lemon juice	Tangy Salad Dressing
	Creamy Orange Salad Dressing

Drain the peaches. Pare the grapefruit and cut crosswise into 6 slices. Peel the banana, slice and sprinkle with lemon juice. Line a serving plate with lettuce and mound strawberries in center of plate. Arrange the peaches and grapefruit in 2 concentric circles around the strawberries. Tuck bundles of banana slices around edge of plate. Serve with salad dressing, Tangy Salad Dressing or Creamy Orange Salad Dressing. 6 servings.

Tangy Salad Dressing

1 c. salad dressing	2 tbsp. chopped green onion
1 tbsp. prepared horseradish	

Mix all ingredients in a bowl.

Creamy Orange Salad Dressing

1 c. salad dressing	2 tbsp. orange marmalade
1/2 c. orange juice	

Mix all ingredients in a bowl.

Peach Symphony Salad (above)

ALMOND-GRAPE SALAD

4 egg yolks	1 lge. can chunk pineapple
Juice of 1 lemon	1 lge. can white grapes
1/4 c. milk	1/2 lb. blanched almonds
1 c. whipping cream, whipped	24 lge. marshmallows, quartered

Beat the egg yolks slightly in top of a double boiler and stir in the lemon juice and milk. Cook over boiling water, stirring, until thick, then remove from water. Cool and fold in the whipped cream. Drain the pineapple and grapes and mix. Add the almonds and marshmallows and fold into dressing. Refrigerate for 24 hours. 8-10 servings.

Mrs. J. R. Holt, Haynesville, Louisiana

GREEN GRAPE SALAD

1/4 c. mayonnaise	Garlic salt to taste
1 3-oz. package cream cheese	1 lb. seedless green grapes

Mix the mayonnaise and cream cheese until smooth and add garlic salt. Fold in the grapes and serve on salad greens. 4-6 servings.

Mrs. Emma L. Van Laningham, Walnut Springs, Texas

TOKAY SALAD

1 3-oz. package cream cheese	Grape leaves or chopped lettuce
1 tbsp. mayonnaise	3/4 lb. Tokay grapes
4 canned or fresh pear halves	

Soften the cream cheese in a bowl and stir in the mayonnaise. Place the pears, cut side down, on grape leaves and cover each pear with cream cheese mixture. Cut the grapes in half and remove seeds. Place the grapes on cheese mixture, cut side down, to cover pears. Serve with additional mayonnaise, if desired. Dip fresh pears in lemon juice to keep from turning brown, if used. 4 servings.

Mrs. Warner Jackson, Stuart, Florida

O'HARA SALAD

2 c. black or white cherries	2 eggs
2 c. diced pineapple	2 tbsp. sugar
2 c. orange sections	1/4 c. light cream
2 c. quartered marshmallows	Juice of 1 lemon
3/4 c. chopped almonds or pecans	1 c. heavy cream, whipped

Drain the cherries, pineapple and orange sections and place in a bowl. Stir in the marshmallows and almonds. Beat the eggs in top of a double boiler until light and add sugar gradually. Add the cream and lemon juice. Cook over boiling water until smooth and thick, stirring constantly. Remove from water and cool. Fold in the whipped cream. Pour over fruit mixture and mix lightly. Chill for 24 hours.

Mrs. M. B. Satterfield, Atlanta, Georgia

AUTUMN'S GOLD SALAD

1 tsp. unflavored gelatin (opt.)	1 1/2 c. shredded Cheddar
2 tbsp. cold water (opt.)	cheese
1 3-oz. package lemon gelatin	2 c. diced unpared red or
1 c. boiling water	golden Delicious apples
1/2 c. sour cream	1/2 c. chopped green pepper
1/4 tsp. dry mustard	1 c. whipping cream, whipped
Lemon juice	Salad greens
1 tbsp. grated onion	Unpared apple slices
1/4 tsp. salt	

Soften the unflavored gelatin in cold water. Combine the lemon gelatin and boiling water in a bowl and stir until gelatin is dissolved. Add the softened gelatin and stir until dissolved. Add the sour cream, mustard, 2 tablespoons lemon juice, onion and salt and beat with rotary beater until smooth. Chill until thickened. Fold in the cheese, diced apples and green pepper, then fold in whipped cream. Spoon into mold which has been rinsed with cold water and chill until firm. Unmold on salad greens and garnish with apple slices which have been dipped in lemon juice to prevent turning brown and additional shredded Cheddar cheese. 8-10 servings.

Autumn's Gold Salad (above)

111

SNOWBALL SALAD

10 canned peach halves
2 3-oz. packages cream cheese
1 3-oz. can candied fruit and
   peels

1/3 c. heavy cream, whipped
1 1/4 c. shredded coconut

Drain the peach halves and dry thoroughly. Mash 1 package cream cheese. Add the candied fruit and peels and mix well. Fill cavities of peach halves with cream cheese mixture and place 2 halves together. Fasten with toothpicks. Mash remaining cream cheese and blend in the whipped cream. Spread on peaches, then roll peaches in coconut. Chill. Serve on crisp lettuce. 5 servings.

Mrs. Elizabeth R. Whisnaut, Spindale, North Carolina

PEACH-PRUNE-COTTAGE CHEESE SALAD

1/4 lb. dried prunes
1 No. 2 can peach halves

1/2 lb. cottage cheese
Crisp lettuce or endive

Soak the prunes overnight in just enough water to cover, then drain. Split on 1 side and remove pits. Drain peaches. Stuff the prunes with cottage cheese and place in cavities of peach halves. Place on lettuce leaves on serving platter. Place remaining cottage cheese in center of platter and serve with mayonnaise, if desired.

Mrs. Sida Mae Womark, Lydowice, Georgia

PEAR-MACAROON SALAD

1 3-oz. package cream cheese
2 tbsp. cream
6 lge. canned or fresh pear
   halves

1/4 c. macaroons, crumbled
Crisp lettuce
6 stemmed maraschino cherries

Mash the cream cheese in a bowl. Add cream and blend thoroughly. Roll round sides of pears in macaroon crumbs. Place pears, cut side up, on lettuce leaves and fill cavities with cheese mixture. Sprinkle top with crumbs and garnish with cherries.

Evelyn Duke, Columbia, Tennessee

FRESH PEAR AND ROQUEFORT SALAD

1 3-oz. package cream cheese
3 tbsp. cream
Salt to taste

3 lge. fresh Bartlett pears
Lemon juice
6 crisp lettuce leaves

1/4 lb. Roquefort cheese   **Paprika**
1/4 c. soft butter

Soften the cream cheese in a bowl. Add the cream and mix until smooth. Season with salt. Peel, core and halve the pears and sprinkle with lemon juice. Arrange the pears, cut side up, on lettuce on individual salad plates. Mix the Roquefort cheese and butter until smooth and place in cavities of the pears. Top with cream cheese mixture and sprinkle with paprika.

Mrs. Bruce Wallace, Asheville, North Carolina

MARINATED PEAR SALAD DELIGHT

3 fresh Bartlett pears	4 tsp. chopped pimento
1 c. salad oil	1/2 tsp. basil
1/4 c. white wine vinegar	6 pitted dates
1/2 tsp. salt	1/4 c. tangy cheese spread
2 tbsp. chopped parsley	Lettuce

Halve and core the pears. Combine remaining ingredients except dates, cheese spread and lettuce in a jar and cover. Shake well. Place pear halves, cut side down, in a shallow bowl and pour vinegar mixture over pears. Cover and refrigerate for 1 hour to 1 hour and 30 minutes. Stuff the dates with cheese spread. Drain pears and reserve marinade. Arrange pears, cut side up, on lettuce-lined serving plate and garnish with dates. Spoon reserved marinade over pears. 6 servings.

Marinated Pear Salad Delight (above)

113

PEAR-TANGERINE SALAD

1 fresh or canned pear, diced	1 tbsp. lime juice
1 c. seeded grapes	1 tsp. salt
2 tangerines, sectioned	Pinch of cayenne pepper
1/2 grapefruit, sectioned	Paprika to taste
1/4 c. olive oil	Curly endive
1 tbsp. lemon juice	Watercress

Combine the pears, grapes, tangerines and grapefruit in a bowl. Combine the oil, lemon juice, lime juice, salt, cayenne pepper and paprika and mix well. Pour over fruits and refrigerate until chilled. Arrange the endive and watercress in a salad bowl and place the fruit mixture on greens.

Mrs. Herman Mueck, Cameron, Texas

PINEAPPLE SANDWICH SALAD

2 tsp. maraschino cherry juice	6 pineapple slices
1 3-oz. package cream cheese	3 lettuce leaves
2 tsp. chopped maraschino	Salad dressing
cherries	Maraschino cherry wedges

Blend the cherry juice into cream cheese in a bowl. Add chopped cherries and mix well. Place a slice of pineapple on each lettuce leaf and spread with cream cheese mixture. Cover with a second slice of pineapple. Top with salad dressing and garnish with cherry wedges. 3 servings.

Mrs. Wilbur C. Johnson, Warrenton, Georgia

STRAWBERRY PATCH SALAD

1 1/2 c. cottage cheese	Lettuce
3 tbsp. mayonnaise	Whole strawberries
1 1/3 c. chopped salted almonds	Mint leaves
3/4 c. strawberry halves	

Combine the cottage cheese and mayonnaise in a bowl. Add the almonds and strawberry halves. Arrange the lettuce in a salad bowl and place cottage cheese mixture on lettuce. Garnish with whole strawberries and mint leaves. Serve with lemon dressing, if desired. 4 servings.

Mrs. Elizabeth Cowley, Saltillo, Mississippi

TANGO

2 peeled bananas, sliced	1/2 c. flaked coconut
Lemon juice	1/2 c. light corn syrup
1 peeled mango, sliced	

Dip the banana slices in lemon juice. Arrange half the banana slices, mango slices and coconut in layers in a salad bowl. Pour 1/4 cup corn syrup over top. Place remaining bananas, mango and coconut in salad bowl and pour remaining corn syrup over all. Chill. Garnish with cherries and strawberries, if desired. 4 servings.

Mrs. Pat Green, Montgomery, Alabama

APRICOT-PINEAPPLE CONGEALED SALAD

1 17-oz. can apricots	2 3-oz. packages orange gelatin
1 env. unflavored gelatin	1 c. pineapple juice
1/2 c. salad dressing	1 lge. can crushed pineapple
1/2 c. sour cream	1 c. miniature marshmallows

Drain the apricots and reserve 1/2 cup syrup. Soften the unflavored gelatin in reserved syrup and dissolve over hot water. Combine the salad dressing and sour cream and stir in gelatin mixture. Pour into a 1 1/2-quart oiled mold and chill until firm. Dissolve the orange gelatin in 2 cups hot water and stir in the pineapple juice and pineapple. Chill until slightly thickened. Chop the apricots and fold into pineapple mixture. Fold in the marshmallows and pour over sour cream mixture. Chill until firm and unmold on greens.

Mrs. Raymond C. Davis, Ellerbe, North Carolina

AVOCADO MOUSSE

1 tbsp. unflavored gelatin	2 tsp. Worcestershire sauce
1/2 c. cold water	2 tbsp. lemon juice
1/2 c. boiling water	2 c. mashed avocado
1 tsp. salt	1/2 c. heavy cream, whipped
1 tsp. onion juice	1/2 c. mayonnaise

Soften the gelatin in cold water and dissolve in boiling water. Add the salt, onion juice, Worcestershire sauce, lemon juice and avocado and chill until thickened. Fold in the whipped cream and mayonnaise and turn into an oiled mold or individual molds. Chill until firm.

Mrs. Mary Belle Nutt, Cotulla, Texas

BLACKBERRY DELIGHT

1 3-oz. package blackberry	1 3-oz. package cream cheese
gelatin	1 carton frozen blackberries
1 c. sugar	1/4 c. chopped nuts
1 c. boiling water	

Dissolve the gelatin and sugar in boiling water in a bowl. Mash the cream cheese. Add 4 tablespoons hot gelatin mixture and mix well. Add the blackberries to remaining gelatin mixture and stir until mixed. Add the nuts and cheese mixture and mix well. Refrigerate until firm.

Mrs. Clarice I. Snider, Erwin, Tennessee

Fresh Banana and Orange Mold (below)

FRESH BANANA AND ORANGE MOLD

1 env. unflavored gelatin	1 1/4 c. fresh orange juice
1/4 c. cold water	2 tbsp. fresh lemon juice
1/4 c. boiling water	2 lge. oranges, sectioned
2 tbsp. sugar	1 lge. banana, sliced
Dash of salt	

Soften the gelatin in cold water and dissolve in boiling water. Add the sugar and salt and stir until completely dissolved. Add fruit juices and chill until slightly thickened. Fold in the orange sections and banana slices and turn into a 3-cup mold or 4 individual molds. Chill until firm. 4 servings.

CHERRY SALAD

1 lge. can Bing cherries	2/3 c. chopped nuts
2 3-oz. packages cherry	2/3 c. chopped celery
gelatin	1 3-oz. package cream cheese
2 1/2 c. cola beverage	

Drain the cherries and reserve juice. Pit the cherries. Heat reserved cherry juice. Add the gelatin and stir until dissolved. Add the cola beverage and mix well. Chill until partially set. Add the cherries, nuts and celery. Crumble the cream cheese and stir into gelatin mixture. Chill until set.

Mrs. Walter McDaniel, Paris, Texas

EGGNOG SALAD

1 No. 2 can crushed pineapple	3 tbsp. fresh lime juice
1 tbsp. unflavored gelatin	1 1/2 c. prepared eggnog

3/4 c. finely chopped celery
1 3-oz. package raspberry
  gelatin
1 1/2 c. boiling water

1 10-oz. package frozen
  cranberry-orange relish,
  thawed

Drain the pineapple syrup into a saucepan and soften the unflavored gelatin in syrup. Add lime juice and heat until gelatin dissolves. Cool. Add the eggnog and chill until partially set. Fold in the pineapple and celery. Turn into a 7-cup salad mold and chill until set. Dissolve the raspberry gelatin in boiling water. Stir in the cranberry-orange relish and chill until partially set. Pour over eggnog layer and chill. 8-10 servings.

Mrs. A. B. Dobson, Duncan, South Carolina

CREAMY GOLDEN WALDORF

1 6-oz. package lemon
  gelatin
1/4 tsp. salt
2/3 c. hot water
2 tbsp. lemon juice
3 med. golden Delicious apples

Lemon juice
1/2 c. mayonnaise
1 c. heavy cream, whipped
1 c. finely chopped celery
1 c. finely chopped walnuts
Salad greens

Dissolve the gelatin and salt in hot water in a bowl and stir in the lemon juice. Chill until thickened. Pare 2 apples partially, then core and dice. Skin will add color to salad. Core and cut remaining apple into thin slices and arrange skin side down, around bottom of 8-cup mold. Sprinkle sliced and diced apples with lemon juice. Blend the mayonnaise into thickened gelatin and fold in the whipped cream. Fold in the diced apples, celery and walnuts gently and spoon over apple slices in mold carefully. Chill until firm. Unmold on salad platter and garnish with greens. 10-12 servings.

Photograph for this recipe on page 98.

APPLE-LIME MOLDS

1 1/2 tbsp. unflavored gelatin
1/3 c. fresh lime juice
1 1/4 c. water
1/2 c. sugar
1/8 tsp. salt

1 tsp. grated lime peel
10 drops of green food coloring
2 med. red Delicious apples
1 c. whipping cream, whipped
Strawberries

Soften the gelatin in lime juice. Heat the water with sugar and salt in a saucepan to simmering. Add the gelatin and stir until dissolved. Stir in the lime peel and food coloring and chill until thickened. Pare and dice 1 apple. Fold the whipped cream into gelatin mixture and fold in the diced apple. Spoon into individual molds and chill until firm. Cut remaining apple into thin slices. Unmold salads and garnish with apple slices and strawberries. Seven 5-ounce molds.

Photograph for this recipe on page 5.

GOOSEBERRY SALAD

1 can gooseberries
1 3-oz. package lemon gelatin
1 c. hot water
1/8 tsp. salt

1 c. miniature marshmallows
1 peeled orange, chopped
1 c. chopped celery
1/2 c. chopped nuts

Drain the gooseberries and reserve juice. Add enough water to reserved juice to make 1 cup liquid. Mix the gelatin with the hot water. Add gooseberry liquid and stir well. Chill until thickened. Add the salt, marshmallows, gooseberries, orange, celery and nuts and chill until firm. Serve on salad greens with mayonnaise, if desired.

Mrs. Velma Trent, Altus, Oklahoma

BLUEBERRY SALAD

1 No. 3 can pineapple chunks
1 No. 2 can blueberries

2 3-oz. packages raspberry gelatin
1/2 c. chopped nuts

Drain the pineapple and blueberries and reserve juices. Combine reserved juices and add enough water to make 3 1/2 cups liquid. Pour into a saucepan and heat. Dissolve gelatin in hot liquid and add the pineapple, blueberries and nuts. Pour into a mold and refrigerate overnight.

Mrs. R. H. Crowder, West Point, Mississippi

LIME-PINEAPPLE SALAD

1 sm. can crushed pineapple
1 pkg. lime gelatin
1 3-oz. package cream cheese
2/3 c. chopped walnuts

2/3 c. chopped celery
1 c. ginger ale
2/3 c. whipping cream

Drain the pineapple and reserve juice. Mix the reserved juice with enough water to make 1 cup liquid and heat to boiling point. Add the gelatin and stir until dissolved. Mash the cream cheese, then stir into gelatin. Add the pineapple, walnuts, celery and ginger ale and refrigerate until thickened. Whip the cream until stiff and fold into gelatin mixture. Pour into a mold and chill until firm. 8-10 servings.

Mrs. Mike Riggs, Laveen, Arizona

MOLDED COTTAGE CHEESE AND PINEAPPLE SALAD

1 env. unflavored gelatin
1 3-oz. package lemon gelatin
1 c. boiling water
1 c. heavy cream, whipped
1 1/2 c. cottage cheese

1 3-oz. package lime gelatin
1 c. pineapple juice, heated
1 c. drained crushed pineapple
1/3 c. sliced stuffed olives
1/3 c. broken walnuts

Soften the unflavored gelatin in 1/4 cup cold water. Add the lemon gelatin and boiling water and stir until dissolved. Chill until thickened, then beat with a rotary beater until light. Fold in the whipped cream and cottage cheese and pour into a mold. Chill until firm. Dissolve the lime gelatin in pineapple juice. Add the pineapple, olives and walnuts and pour onto congealed layer. Chill until firm. 12 servings.

Mrs. Jack Henson, Sylva, North Carolina

ORANGE SALAD MOLD

2 3-oz. packages orange gelatin
2 c. hot water
1 c. orange juice
1 1/2 c. orange sherbet

2 c. sweetened strawberries, drained
1 1/2 c. sour cream

Dissolve the gelatin in hot water. Add the orange juice and mix thoroughly. Fold in sherbet and whip until smooth. Turn into a mold and chill until firm. Mix remaining ingredients. Place the salad on lettuce and top with sour cream mixture.

Mrs. S. S. Nichols, Meridian, Texas

PEACH-GINGER ALE SALAD

1 3-oz. package strawberry gelatin
1/4 tsp. salt
1 c. hot water

1 c. ginger ale
1 No. 2 1/2 can peach halves, drained
Lettuce

Dissolve the gelatin and salt in hot water. Add the ginger ale and chill until slightly thickened. Place the peach halves in a 9-inch square pan and pour the gelatin over peaches. Chill until firm. Cut into squares and serve on lettuce leaves. Garnish with salad dressing and cream cheese balls rolled in chopped nuts. 6 servings.

Mrs. L. D. Grimes, Maud, Texas

SPICED PEACH SOUFFLE SALAD

1 No. 2 1/2 can sliced peaches
1 3-oz. package orange gelatin
1/2 c. chopped celery
1/2 c. chopped pecans

1/4 c. mayonnaise
1 c. evaporated milk
2 tbsp. lemon juice

Drain the peaches and reserve 1 cup syrup. Chop the peaches and chill. Heat reserved syrup in a saucepan to boiling point and remove from heat. Add the gelatin and stir until dissolved. Pour into a large bowl and chill until the consistency of unbeaten egg white. Stir in the celery, pecans and mayonnaise. Freeze the milk in refrigerator tray until ice crystals form around edge. Place in a small, well-chilled bowl and add lemon juice. Beat until stiff. Fold into gelatin mixture and spoon into an oiled 6-cup mold. Chill until firm. 6-8 servings.

Mrs. Orvil Huskey, Strawberry, Arkansas

RASPBERRY BAVARIAN MOLD

1 10-oz. package frozen red raspberries, thawed	1 tbsp. lemon juice
	Dash of salt
1 3-oz. package raspberry gelatin	1 6-oz. can evaporated milk, chilled
1 c. hot water	

Drain the raspberries and reserve syrup. Dissolve the gelatin in hot water. Add reserved syrup, lemon juice and salt and mix well. Chill until partially set. Add the milk and beat with electric mixer at high speed until fluffy. Fold in the raspberries and pour into a 1 1/2-quart mold. Chill until firm.

Mrs. Lester Burgess, New Braunfels, Texas

RASPBERRY-CRANBERRY SALAD

1 3-oz. package raspberry gelatin	1 jar cranberry relish
	1 c. miniature marshmallows
1 8-oz. package cream cheese, softened	1 c. chopped nuts

Prepare the gelatin according to package directions. Add the cream cheese and stir until mixed. Chill until thickened. Stir in the relish, marshmallows and nuts and refrigerate until firm.

Mrs. Nadean Holley, Eclectic, Alabama

SPICY SALAD

1 cinnamon stick	1/2 c. diced celery
1 3-oz. package lemon gelatin	1/4 c. chopped peanuts
1/2 c. diced apple	

Pour 1 1/4 cups water into a saucepan. Add the cinnamon stick and bring to a boil. Simmer for 10 minutes. Add enough hot water to make 1 cup liquid, if needed. Add gelatin and stir until dissolved. Add 1 cup cold water and stir well. Remove cinnamon stick. Chill until slightly thickened. Fold in the apple, celery and peanuts and pour into a mold. Chill until firm.

Mrs. Edna Chadsey, Corpus Christi, Texas

RED AND GREEN RIBBON RING

1 3-oz. package strawberry gelatin	1 c. crushed pineapple
	1/4 c. chopped pecans (opt.)
1 1-lb. can whole cranberry sauce	1 3-oz. package lime gelatin
1 3-oz. package lemon gelatin	2 tbsp. sugar
1 8-oz. package cream cheese, softened	2 c. grapefruit sections

Dissolve the strawberry gelatin in 1 cup boiling water. Add the cranberry sauce and mix well. Chill until partially set. Pour into an 8-cup ring mold and chill until almost firm. Dissolve the lemon gelatin in 1 cup boiling water. Add the cream cheese and beat with rotary beater until mixed. Add pineapple and chill until partially set. Stir in the pecans and pour over cranberry layer in mold. Chill until almost firm. Dissolve the lime gelatin and sugar in 1 1/4 cup boiling water and stir in the grapefruit. Chill until partially set. Pour over cheese layer and chill until firm. 10-12 servings.

Mrs. Nettie Searcy, Pleasant Shade, Tennessee

COTTAGE CHEESE AND FRUIT MOLD

1 6-oz. package lemon gelatin	Orange sections
1 c. boiling water	Whole strawberries
1 6-oz. can frozen orange	Avocado crescents
juice concentrate	Pineapple spears
1 tsp. salt	Grapefruit sections
1 lb. cream-style cottage	Apricot halves
cheese	Salad greens
2 c. sour cream	Salad dressing

Dissolve the gelatin in boiling water. Add the orange juice concentrate and salt and stir until blended. Chill until slightly thickened. Whip the cottage cheese until smooth and combine with the sour cream. Fold into gelatin mixture and place in a 6-cup ring mold. Chill until firm. Unmold on a large salad or cake plate and arrange desired fresh fruits and sprigs of salad greens around the outside border. Serve with desired salad dressing. 12 servings.

Cottage Cheese and Fruit Mold (above)

Nectarine Salad Olivera (page 124)

combination fruit & vegetable salads

Take the tartness or sweetness of fruit ripened under the southern sun . . . add the rich flavor of vegetables grown in some of the finest soil in the country . . . mix them in a salad bowl . . . add a complementary dressing – and you have fruit and vegetable salads – combinations *Southern Living* homemakers love to prepare!

These are women who know that their region grows a variety of the best vegetables and fruits in the nation – produce which is available in their markets at low cost. They take advantage of this bounty to serve their appreciative family and guests a collection of the most flavorful salads to be found on any dinner table – anywhere!

And in the pages that follow, you'll find the very best of these fruit-and-vegetable combination salads. Look, for instance, at the recipe for Avocado-Vegetable Medley. It's almost certain to become as much a favorite with your family as it is with the family of the southern homemaker who shares it with you in this section. From the southernmost tip of the Southland has come Key West Salad – a lively blend of flavors that perks up every meal. And at your next buffet party, try serving Mexican Salad. It is congealed – and easy to handle – and the sparkling blend of flavors will add new dimensions to your menu!

These are recipes you'll turn to again and again when you want to surprise your family and friends with flavorful fruit and vegetable salads!

ALL-GREEN SALAD

1 1-lb. can green beans	2 c. torn fresh spinach
1/2 c. French dressing	1/2 tsp. curry powder (opt.)
1 sm. head lettuce	1 avocado, diced

Drain the green beans and add the French dressing. Refrigerate for 2 hours. Tear the lettuce into a salad bowl and add spinach. Drain the green beans, reserving dressing. Add curry powder to reserved dressing and shake well. Add green beans and avocado to the salad and toss, using only enough dressing to moisten. Garnish with crushed dry-roasted peanuts, chopped hard-cooked egg or grated Swiss cheese, if desired. 4-6 servings.

Mrs. C. Ed. Gardner, Pennington Gap, Virginia

APPLE-COCONUT AND CELERY SALAD

1 c. diced tart apples	4 tbsp. orange juice
1/2 c. diced celery	Salt to taste
1/2 c. shredded coconut	Paprika to taste
1 tbsp. lemon juice	Lettuce leaves
1 tbsp. sugar	Currant or plum jelly
4 tbsp. salad oil	

Combine the apples, celery and coconut and toss. Sprinkle the lemon juice and sugar over the top. Mix the oil, orange juice, salt and paprika, then pour over the salad. Chill. Line the salad bowl with lettuce leaves and pile the salad in the center. Dot with currant or plum jelly. 3-4 servings.

Mrs. Alvin G. Kouts, Montgomery, Alabama

NECTARINE SALAD OLIVERA

2 1-lb. cans red kidney beans	1 tsp. sugar
1/2 c. pitted ripe olives, halved	1 tsp. crumbled oregano
1/4 c. chopped onion	1/2 tsp. salt
1/3 c. salad or olive oil	1 clove of garlic, minced
6 tbsp. Chianti	2 c. sliced fresh nectarines
1/4 c. wine vinegar	1 avocado, cut in cubes

Drain the beans and place in a bowl. Add the olives, onion, oil, Chianti, vinegar, sugar, oregano, salt and garlic and toss well. Chill. Add the nectarines and avocado and toss lightly. Garnish with green onions or tiny romaine leaves poking out of center, if desired. Other red wine may be substituted for Chianti. 10-12 servings.

Photograph for this recipe on page 122.

APPLE-CABBAGE SLAW

1/2 med. cabbage, shredded	Salt and pepper to taste
1 red apple, chopped	2 sm. carrots, cut in rings
1/2 c. raisins	1 c. salad dressing
1 stalk celery, chopped	6 maraschino cherries, chopped

Combine all the ingredients and mix, then chill well. 6 servings.

Mrs. Emmett B. Bell, New Boston, Texas

AVOCADO SALAD MONTEREY

1 3-oz. package cream cheese	1/4 c. salad oil
2 avocados, halved lengthwise	2 tbsp. vinegar
Lemon juice	1 tbsp. finely chopped onion
6 c. bite-sized salad greens	1 tsp. salt
1 peeled tomato, cut in	1/8 tsp. seasoned pepper
wedges	1/4 tsp. chili powder
1 c. sliced cooked zucchini	1/4 tsp. sugar
2 green chili peppers, sliced	

Cut the cream cheese in 1/2-inch cubes. Remove avocado seeds and peel avocados. Slice into quarters and sprinkle with lemon juice. Line a salad bowl with salad greens. Arrange avocados, tomato, cream cheese, zucchini and chili peppers over greens. Combine remaining ingredients in a jar and cover. Shake to blend. Pour over salad and toss lightly just before serving. One cup well-drained canned pear tomatoes and 1 cup cut Blue Lake green beans may be substituted for tomato and zucchini, if desired. 8 servings.

Avocado Salad Monterey (above)

125

FRENCH AVOCADO SALAD

2 avocados, diced
3 hard-cooked eggs, diced
3 sm. tomatoes, diced
6 stuffed olives, sliced
1 sm. onion, minced

French dressing
Chili powder to taste
Crisp lettuce
Fried bacon slices

Combine the avocados, eggs, tomatoes, olives and onion, then mix. Add enough French dressing to moisten and season with chili powder. Serve on lettuce leaves with bacon. 6 servings.

Mrs. George Veith, Louisville, Kentucky

AVOCADO-VEGETABLE MEDLEY

1 10-oz. package cooked frozen
   peas, drained
1 med. cucumber, sliced
1/2 c. sliced green onions or
   scallions
1/2 c. French dressing

1 avocado, sliced
1/4 c. lemon juice
1/2 tsp. salt
Salad greens
1 c. coarsely grated carrots

Combine peas, cucumber, onions and dressing, then toss. Cover and chill for about 2 hours. Marinate the avocado in lemon juice and salt for 30 minutes. Line a salad bowl with salad greens and spoon the pea mixture into a bowl. Arrange the avocado slices in ring around edge and place carrots in center. 6 servings.

Mrs. I. C. O'Brien, St. Petersburg, Florida

BACON AND APPLE SALAD

6 slices bacon
4 med. apples, diced
2 c. chopped celery

2 hard-cooked eggs, chopped
Mayonnaise

Fry the bacon until crisp, then drain and break into pieces. Combine with the apples, celery and eggs and moisten with mayonnaise. Toss lightly and serve.

Mrs. Odell Wells, Philadelphia, Mississippi

CABBAGE-CARROT SALAD

1/2 c. raisins
1/3 c. drained crushed pineapple
1/4 c. mayonnaise

1/2 med. head cabbage, shredded
2 lge. carrots, shredded
Salt and pepper to taste

Combine all the ingredients and mix well.

Mrs. Chris Eberlan, San Augustine, Texas

CAULIFLOWER AND APPLE SALAD

1 sm. cauliflower, thinly sliced	1/4 c. red wine vinegar
3 apples, diced	1/4 c. olive or salad oil
1 c. sliced celery	1/2 tsp. salt
4 sm. green onions, sliced	Dash of white pepper
1/2 c. chopped parsley	1 bunch watercress

Combine the cauliflower, apples, celery, onions and parsley, then chill. Combine the vinegar, oil, salt and pepper in a tightly covered jar and shake. Pour over the salad and toss lightly. Garnish with watercress. 6 servings.

Mrs. Chris Jacobs, Topeka, Kansas

GLORIFIED WALDORF SALAD

1 tbsp. lemon juice	1 c. chopped nuts
2 c. chopped apples	1 c. chopped dates
1 c. chopped avocado	Sour cream to taste
1 c. diced celery	

Sprinkle the lemon juice over apples and avocado and add the celery, nuts and dates. Add enough sour cream to moisten and toss.

Dressing

1 c. sour cream	1/2 tsp. salt
1 tsp. wine vinegar	1 tsp. sugar
1 tsp. prepared mustard	

Combine all the ingredients and mix well. Serve with the salad.

Mrs. Henry Sherrer, Bay City, Texas

HOME GARDEN MARINADE

Radish slices	3/4 c. fresh lime juice
Sweet onion rings	6 tbsp. olive oil
Cucumber sticks	1 sm. garlic clove, crushed
Thinly sliced tomatoes	1 1/2 tbsp. sugar
Green pepper rings	1 1/2 tsp. salt
Avocado slices	1/2 tsp. pepper
Carrot curls	1 tsp. aromatic bitters

Arrange the first 7 ingredients on a platter and refrigerate for 1 hour. Combine the remaining ingredients in covered jar or blender and mix well. Pour over the vegetable platter. 8 servings.

Mrs. Odell T. Lakeman, Haleyville, Alabama

HEARTS OF PALM SALAD A LA DE VERA

1 c. finely diced pineapple	2 tbsp. crunchy peanut butter
4 c. sliced hearts of palm	2 tbsp. mayonnaise
1/4 c. chopped dates	Few drops of green food coloring
1/4 c. chopped candied ginger	1 to 2 tbsp. pineapple juice
1/4 c. vanilla ice cream	

Combine the pineapple, hearts of palm, dates and ginger in a salad bowl and toss. Combine the ice cream, peanut butter, mayonnaise and green food coloring to tint a pale green and blend well. Add the pineapple juice to thin to desired consistency and pour dressing over the salad.

Mrs. Bessie Gibbs, Cedar Key, Florida

SPICY BEAN-APPLE SALAD

1 1-lb. can cut Blue Lake green beans	6 whole cloves
3 tbsp. vinegar	1/4 tsp. salt
1 tbsp. chopped candied ginger	2 c. chopped tart red apples
1 2-in. stick cinnamon	1/4 c. raisins
	1/3 c. red onion rings

Drain the beans, reserving 1/2 cup liquid. Combine reserved liquid with vinegar, ginger, cinnamon, cloves and salt in a saucepan and bring to a boil. Stir in apples and raisins and cook over medium heat for about 5 minutes or until apples are tender-crisp. Add the beans and onion rings and bring to a boil. Remove from heat. Pour into a bowl and serve hot. May be covered and refrigerated until chilled. 5-6 servings.

Spicy Bean-Apple Salad (above)

KIDNEY BEAN-APPLE SALAD

2 1/2 c. canned kidney beans
3/4 c. diced tart apple
1/2 c. chopped sweet pickle
1/2 c. chopped cabbage

Paprika
1/2 tsp. salt
Mayonnaise

Drain the beans and add the remaining ingredients with enough mayonnaise to blend. Chill, then serve on crisp lettuce.

Mrs. R. C. Bouse, Jr., Port Bolivar, Texas

KEY WEST SALAD

2 Bermuda onions, sliced
Cream cheese balls
Paprika

Lettuce
4 lge. oranges, sectioned
1/2 c. French dressing

Cut onion slices in half. Roll the cream cheese balls in paprika and place on the lettuce. Arrange the onion and orange sections, petal fashion, around cream cheese ball. Drizzle the dressing over top. 4 servings.

Mrs. Harry Anderson, Daytona, Florida

LETTUCE AND BANANA SALAD

Lemon juice
1 lge. banana, sliced
1/4 c. finely diced onion
1 sm. head lettuce, shredded

1/8 tsp. garlic powder
Salt and pepper to taste
1/3 c. mayonnaise

Sprinkle lemon juice on the banana and combine all the ingredients except the mayonnaise. Add the mayonnaise just before serving. 6 servings.

Mrs. H. W. Moore, Ft. Stewart, Georgia

LOGROLLER'S SALAD

2 tbsp. lemon juice
4 c. chopped red apples
4 c. cooked navy beans, drained
1 c. chopped green pepper

1 c. chopped sweet onion
1 tsp. salt
2 tbsp. sugar
2 tbsp. salad dressing

Add the lemon juice to the apples to prevent discoloring. Combine all ingredients and mix, then chill. Serve on lettuce. 6 servings.

Mrs. C. L. Speak, Springdale, Arkansas

LETTUCE-AVOCADO DELIGHT

3 to 4 heads Bibb lettuce
1/2 head iceberg lettuce
2 avocados, sliced
3 hard-cooked eggs, sliced

1/2 lb. bacon, fried and crumbled
1 can mandarin oranges, drained
1/2 c. slivered almonds
1 env. bleu cheese dressing mix

Tear the lettuce into bite-sized pieces and add the remaining ingredients except the dressing mix. Chill. Prepare the dressing mix according to package directions and pour desired amount over salad. Toss. 6-8 servings.

Mrs. Charles Sieman, Jacksonville, Florida

LUAU COLESLAW

2 tsp. sugar
3/4 c. mayonnaise
1/4 c. vinegar
1 tsp. salt
Fresh or ground pepper to taste

3 qt. finely shredded cabbage
1 6-oz. can chilled cranberry
   sauce, cut in cubes
1 11-oz. can mandarin oranges,
   drained

Combine the sugar, mayonnaise, vinegar, salt and pepper, then mix and chill. Combine the cabbage, cranberry cubes and orange sections, then add the dressing mixture. Toss until evenly coated. 6-8 servings.

Mrs. B. E. North, Atlanta, Georgia

MANDARIN SALAD WITH SESAME DRESSING

1 head lettuce
1 bunch watercress
1 cucumber, thinly sliced
1 11-oz. can mandarin oranges,
   drained

1/4 c. salad oil
2 tbsp. cider vinegar
1 tbsp. sugar
1 tsp. soy sauce
1 tsp. sesame seed

Break the lettuce and watercress into bite-sized pieces. Arrange the cucumber and orange slices on top. Combine the remaining ingredients in a jar and shake well. Drizzle with dressing and toss lightly just before serving. 6 servings.

Mrs. R. M. Kennell, Hampton, Virginia

MILLIONAIRE'S SALAD

1 No. 2 can hearts of palm
1 No. 2 can pineapple chunks,
   drained

1 ripe avocado, cut up
1 c. salad dressing
1 tsp. sugar

Cut the hearts of palm into bite-sized pieces and combine with the remaining ingredients. Serve in lettuce cups. 8 servings.

Mrs. Diane Searcy, Tifton, Georgia

MOUNTAINEER SALAD

2 c. shredded cabbage
1 c. miniature marshmallows
1 c. green grapes
1/2 c. raisins

1/2 c. shredded coconut
1/2 c. chopped nuts
1/4 c. heavy cream

Combine all the ingredients and toss until well moistened. Chill. 6-8 servings.

Mrs. J. M. Allen, San Angelo, Texas

GREEN AND GOLD SALAD

1/2 c. olive oil
2 tbsp. red wine vinegar
1 tbsp. lemon juice
1 clove of garlic, halved
1 tbsp. chopped parsley
1 tsp. dry mustard
1 tsp. salt
Pepper to taste

2 fully ripe avocados
6 c. torn lettuce
4 c. torn spinach
1 c. sliced stuffed olives
2 lge. peeled oranges,
    sectioned
1/2 red onion, thinly sliced

Combine the oil, vinegar, lemon juice, garlic, parsley, mustard, salt and pepper in a jar and cover. Shake well and chill. Halve avocados lengthwise just before serving, twisting gently to separate halves. Whack a sharp knife directly into seeds and twist to lift out. Peel the avocados. Place, cavity side down, on a flat surface and slice. Arrange avocado slices and remaining ingredients in a salad bowl. Add the dressing and toss lightly. Avocados may be ripened at room temperature until soft to the touch. 6-8 servings.

Green and Gold Salad (above)

PINEAPPLE BEETS

1 13 1/2-oz. can pineapple chunks	1/2 tsp. salt
1/3 c. cider vinegar	1/8 tsp. ground ginger
4 tbsp. sugar	2 1-lb. cans sliced beets, drained
1 tbsp. cornstarch	

Drain the pineapple and reserve the syrup. Combine 1/2 cup water, vinegar and reserved syrup. Mix the sugar, cornstarch, salt and ginger and add the vinegar mixture. Cook until thickened, stirring constantly. Add the beets and bring to a boil, then stir in the pineapple. Cool and serve on lettuce. 8 servings.

Mrs. Arley A. Sarver, Crowley, Louisiana

RED CABBAGE-ORANGE SALAD

1 sm. red cabbage, shredded	Dash of salt
3 med. oranges, sectioned	3/4 c. cottage cheese
1/4 c. chopped chives	Juice of 1 orange
1/4 green pepper, slivered	

Combine cabbage, orange sections, chives, green pepper and salt. Combine the cottage cheese and orange juice, then mix into cabbage mixture. Serve on lettuce and garnish with slivers of green pepper and orange peel, if desired.

Mrs. Mattie Butler, Alexandria, Louisiana

SALAD OF THE ISLANDS

Lettuce	3 tbsp. lemon juice
4 c. cubed fresh pineapple	3 tbsp. catsup
2 c. cubed tomatoes	1/2 c. light cream
1 tbsp. grated onion	Salt and pepper to taste

Line a salad bowl with lettuce and add the pineapple and tomatoes. Sprinkle with onion. Combine the remaining ingredients and mix well. Pour over the salad. 6 servings.

Mrs. James R. Payne, Moultrie, Georgia

SANTA ROSA SALAD

3 cucumbers	Garlic
1 lb. seedless green grapes	Sour Cream Dressing
2 or 3 bunches watercress	

Peel and slice the cucumbers, leaving some of the green peel. Cover the slices with ice cubes and water and refrigerate to crisp. Wash and remove the stems from the grapes. Wash and dry the watercress. Rub a chilled salad bowl with garlic just before serving. Drain and dry the cucumbers and place in bowl with grapes and watercress. Toss with the Sour Cream Dressing.

Sour Cream Dressing

2/3 c. salad oil	1 tbsp. sugar
1/3 c. wine vinegar	1 tsp. paprika
6 tbsp. sour cream	1/2 tsp. dry mustard
1 tsp. salt	1/8 tsp. red pepper

Combine all the ingredients in jar and shake well. Chill.

Mrs. Grady Gilbert, Robertsdale, Alabama

SPANISH ORANGE SALAD

1 lge. head lettuce	1 green pepper, cut in rings
2 lge. oranges, peeled and sliced	2 tbsp. olive oil
	1 tbsp. vinegar
1 cucumber, thinly sliced	1/2 tsp. salt
1 sm. onion, cut in rings	

Arrange the lettuce in a salad bowl and stand the orange slices on edge among the greens with cucumber slices in between. Place onion and green pepper rings over the top. Combine the olive oil, vinegar and salt and pour over salad. 4 servings.

Emily Filipi, Mobile, Alabama

STUFFED PRUNE AND ORANGE SALAD

12 lge. cooked prunes	1 stalk celery, finely chopped
Mayonnaise	3 lge. oranges

Remove pits from the prunes. Mix a small amount of mayonnaise with the celery and stuff into prunes. Pare the oranges and slice crosswise. Arrange 3 slices of orange in center of a lettuce leaf. Place a prune on both sides of orange slices. Serve with desired dressing. Endive may be substituted for lettuce. 6 servings.

Mrs. M. L. Shannon, Fairfield, Alabama

WEST INDIAN SALAD

2 avocados, halved and pared	Juice of 1 lemon
Shredded lettuce	Salt and pepper to taste
1 cucumber, coarsely grated	1 tbsp. olive oil

Place the avocados on lettuce. Season the cucumber with lemon juice, salt, pepper and olive oil. Fill avocados with cucumber mixture. 4 servings.

Mrs. James K. Hess, New Orleans, Louisiana

Hot Pineapple-Yam Salad (below)

HOT PINEAPPLE-YAM SALAD

1 13 1/2-oz. can pineapple tidbits	1/4 tsp. dry mustard
6 strips bacon	1/2 tsp. salt
1/3 c. chopped onion	1 tsp. flour
1/2 c. thinly sliced celery	1 tbsp. cider vinegar
2 tbsp. chopped green pepper	1 lb. yams, boiled in jackets

Drain the pineapple and reserve 1/4 cup syrup. Cut the bacon in 1-inch slices and cook in a skillet until crisp. Remove from skillet and keep warm. Drain off all except 2 tablespoons bacon drippings from skillet. Saute the onion, celery and green pepper in the bacon drippings in skillet until tender. Add the mustard, salt, flour, reserved pineapple syrup and vinegar and cook for several minutes. Add pineapple tidbits and cover. Keep warm. Peel and slice the yams. Add to the pineapple mixture and toss lightly. Top with bacon. 6 servings.

SOUR CREAM FRUIT SALAD IN COCONUT NESTS

2 c. shredded coconut	1/2 c. halved green grapes
1/2 c. powdered sugar	1/2 c. drained pineapple tidbits
2 tsp. green food coloring	1/2 c. miniature marshmallows
1/2 tsp. water	2 tbsp. chopped nuts
3 tbsp. melted butter	2 tbsp. sour cream
1/2 c. diced celery	
1/2 c. chopped red apple	

Mix the coconut and sugar in a 2-quart jar. Combine the food coloring and water and sprinkle over coconut mixture. Cover jar and shake vigorously to tint coconut. Mix tinted coconut with melted butter. Spoon into 6 muffin cups and mold to form nests. Refrigerate for at least 1 hour. Dip muffin pan into lukewarm water and lift out nests. Combine remaining ingredients and spoon into coconut nests.

Mrs. Alvin Reid, Pilot Mountain, North Carolina

SALAD ROYALE

1 qt. shredded cabbage	1/2 c. (scant) mayonnaise
3 peach halves, diced	1/2 c. (scant) sugar
1/2 c. pineapple chunks	1/4 c. heavy cream, whipped
6 maraschino cherries, diced	

Combine the first 4 ingredients and chill. Combine the remaining ingredients and mix, then toss with the salad just before serving.

Mrs. Emil W. Merritt, Greensboro, North Carolina

APPLE AND GRAPEFRUIT SALAD

4 crisp lettuce leaves	1/4 c. pecan halves
24 grapefruit sections	2 to 3 tbsp. mayonnaise
French dressing	16 strips green pepper
3 red Delicious apples	4 sprigs of fresh mint

Place the lettuce leaves on individual salad plates and arrange the grapefruit sections on lettuce. Add small amount of French dressing. Wash and core the apples and cut in cubes. Add the pecans and enough mayonnaise to moisten and mix well. Place on grapefruit. Garnish with green pepper and mint.

Wilma Mansel, West Columbia, Texas

ARTICHOKE-GRAPEFRUIT SALAD

1 head crisp lettuce	2 grapefruit, sectioned
1 bunch endive	Garlic dressing or Roquefort
2 onions, sliced	dressing
1 can artichoke hearts, drained	

Tear the lettuce and endive into bite-sized pieces into a large salad bowl and toss. Separate the onion slices into rings and place on top. Add the artichoke hearts and grapefruit sections. Pour desired amount of dressing over top. 6 servings.

Monna S. Ray, Alexandria, Virginia

135

VARIATION GUACAMOLE SALAD

1 med. onion, peeled
2 med. tomatoes, peeled
Dash of cayenne pepper
1 clove of garlic, crushed

2 tsp. salt
2 avocados, mashed
2 tbsp. lemon juice

Grind the onion and tomatoes together and blend in the pepper, garlic and salt. Add the avocados and lemon juice. Serve on shredded lettuce.

Mrs. Lena Nitcholos, Idalou, Texas

COTTAGE CHEESE AND PINEAPPLE SALAD MOLD

1 No. 2 can crushed pineapple
2 env. unflavored gelatin
1 pt. cottage cheese
3/4 c. mayonnaise
1 tbsp. sugar

1 c. broken pecans
1/4 c. diced green pepper
1/2 c. diced celery
1 sm. can pimento, chopped
1/2 pt. heavy cream, whipped

Drain the syrup from the pineapple and add the gelatin to the syrup, then soften for 5 minutes. Dissolve over hot water. Add the pineapple, cottage cheese, mayonnaise, sugar, pecans, green pepper, celery and pimento, then fold in the whipped cream. Turn into a mold and chill overnight or until firm. 12 servings.

Mrs. A. M. Carney, Nashville, Tennessee

CRANBERRY-NUT SALAD

1 lb. cranberries, ground
1 c. sugar
1 No. 2 can crushed pineapple
1 c. chopped celery

1 c. chopped pecans
12 lge. marshmallows, cut in
   sm. pieces
2 pkg. cherry gelatin

Combine the cranberries and sugar and set aside for several minutes. Add the pineapple, celery, pecans and marshmallows. Dissolve the gelatin in 2 cups hot water, then add 1 cup cold water. Pour over the cranberry mixture and mix. Chill until set. Serve on lettuce and garnish with mayonnaise.

Mrs. W. A. Howard, Chattanooga, Tennessee

FALCON'S NEST SALAD

1 1/2 c. evaporated milk
1 3-oz. package lemon gelatin
1 3-oz. package lime gelatin
2 c. hot water
1 1/2 c. crushed pineapple
2 tbsp. lemon juice

1/2 c. diced celery
2 tsp. horseradish
1 c. salad dressing
1 c. chopped nuts
1/2 lb. cottage cheese

Freeze the evaporated milk in a pan until ice crystals form around edge. Whip until stiff. Dissolve the lemon and lime gelatins in hot water in a bowl and stir in the pineapple and lemon juice. Fold in the whipped milk and remaining ingredients and place in a mold. Chill until firm.

Mrs. Winnie Vinson, Erin, Tennessee

FESTIVE WALNUT SALAD

3/4 c. chopped walnuts	1/4 tsp. salt
1 c. fresh cranberries	1 8 1/2-oz. can pineapple
1/4 c. sugar	tidbits
2 3-oz. packages lemon	1 10-oz. bottle lemon-lime
gelatin	carbonated beverage, chilled
1 3/4 c. boiling water	1 c. finely chopped celery
3 tbsp. lemon juice	1 8-oz. package cream cheese

Place the walnuts in a baking pan. Bake at 300 degrees for about 10 minutes or until toasted. Set aside. Chop the cranberries coarsely and mix with sugar. Let stand while preparing salad. Dissolve the gelatin in boiling water, then stir in the lemon juice and salt. Drain the pineapple and reserve syrup. Pour reserved syrup into gelatin mixture and cool thoroughly. Stir in the carbonated beverage and chill until thickened. Reserve 1 1/2 cups for cheese layer. Stir the cranberry mixture, pineapple, celery and 1/2 of the walnuts into remaining gelatin mixture. Spoon into a 6-cup mold and chill until almost set. Soften the cream cheese and blend in reserved gelatin gradually. Stir in the walnuts and spoon onto cranberry mixture. Chill until firm. Unmold onto salad greens. About 8 servings.

Festive Walnut Salad (above)

MEXICAN SALAD

1 pkg. lemon gelatin
1 1/2 c. hot water
2 tsp. sugar
1 tsp. salt
1/4 c. white vinegar
1/8 tsp. chili powder

1 c. finely shredded cabbage
1/2 c. finely chopped celery
1 4-oz. jar pimento strips
1/2 c. green pepper strips
1 med. red apple, chopped

Dissolve the gelatin in hot water and blend in the sugar, salt, vinegar and chili powder. Cool until slightly thickened, then add the remaining ingredients. Chill until firm.

Mrs. Jane Willis, Beaumont, Texas

RHUBARB-PINEAPPLE SALAD

1 pkg. frozen rhubarb
2 tbsp. sugar
1 pkg. raspberry gelatin
1 c. pineapple juice

1 tsp. lemon juice
1 c. diced apples
1 c. diced celery
1/4 c. chopped pecans

Prepare the rhubarb according to package directions, adding the sugar and cooking until tender. Stir the gelatin into the hot rhubarb, then add the pineapple and lemon juices. Cool until thickened. Add the apples, celery and pecans and pour into individual molds. Chill until firm. 6 servings.

Mrs. Hobert Collins, Knoxville, Tennessee

CHERRY SALAD

1 env. unflavored gelatin
1 can sour pitted cherries
Juice of 2 oranges
Juice of 1 lemon
1 pkg. lemon gelatin

1 c. sugar
Grated rind of 1 orange
1 c. chopped celery
1 c. chopped pecans

Soften the unflavored gelatin in 1/4 cup cold water. Drain the juice from the cherries and add the orange juice and lemon juice. Bring to a boil and add the gelatins and sugar. Stir until dissolved, then cool until thickened. Fold in cherries, orange rind, celery and pecans and chill until firm.

Frances Rife, Richmond, Virginia

VERSATILE SALAD

1 6-oz. package orange gelatin
1 3-oz. package lemon gelatin
1 No. 2 can pears
1 No. 2 can crushed pineapple

3/4 c. mayonnaise or salad
   dressing
1 c. diced celery
1/2 c. grated coconut
1 c. chopped nuts

Dissolve the gelatins in 3 cups hot water and cool. Drain the pears and pineapple and reserve juices. Mix reserved juices and add enough water to make 3 cups liquid. Stir into the gelatin and chill until consistency of unbeaten egg whites. Chop the pears and add to gelatin. Add the pineapple and remaining ingredients and chill until firm.

Mrs. Dorothy S. Sims, Lamar, South Carolina

LIME AVOCADO SALAD

1 pkg. lime gelatin
2 pkg. cream cheese
2 avocados
1/2 c. mayonnaise

1 sm. can pimento, chopped
1/4 green pepper, chopped
Grated onion to taste

Dissolve the gelatin in 1 cup hot water. Blend the cream cheese and avocados together and add the gelatin and remaining ingredients. Mix well and chill until firm. 6 servings.

Mrs. Francis Smith, Abilene, Texas

HARLEQUIN CHEESE-APPLE SALAD

2 env. unflavored gelatin
1 1/2 c. water
1 can Cheddar cheese soup
1/2 c. salad dressing
1/2 c. milk

1 tsp. salt
2 red apples, diced
1/2 c. diced celery
1/2 c. minced green pepper

Sprinkle the gelatin on the water in a saucepan and let soften for 5 minutes. Place over low heat and stir until gelatin is dissolved. Blend the soup and salad dressing until smooth in large bowl, then stir in the milk, salt and gelatin. Chill until slightly thickened, then fold in the remaining ingredients. Pour into a 5-cup mold and chill until firm.

Mrs. J. W. Hopkins, Abilene, Texas

FRUIT AND CHEESE RING

1 No. 2 can crushed pineapple
1 3-oz. package lemon gelatin
1/2 c. mayonnaise

1 5-oz. jar pimento cheese
   spread
1 c. grated carrots

Drain the pineapple, reserving 3/4 cup syrup. Dissolve the gelatin in 1 cup hot water and add the mayonnaise and pimento cheese. Beat until smooth with electric or rotary beater. Stir in the reserved pineapple juice, then chill until partially set. Fold in carrots and pineapple and turn into 5 1/2-cup ring mold. Chill until firm. Unmold and fill with grapes or other fruit. 6 servings.

Mrs. J. T. Nagle, Paris, Kentucky

Macaroni-Tuna Lunch Box Salad (page 154)

cheese, egg, cereal & pasta salads

Vegetables, fruit, meat, and seafood all can be mixed and matched to make unforgettable salads. But innovative southern cooks have gone beyond these foods and developed many exciting recipes which turn cheese, eggs, cereal, and pasta into equally memorable salads. Who but a southern homemaker would have combined the mild smoothness of cottage cheese with the peppery bite of watercress in Cottage Cheese with Watercress?

A *Southern Living* cook did — and her recipe is just one of the many awaiting you in the section that follows. Here you'll find such staples as macaroni ... rice ... cottage cheese ... hard-cooked eggs ... noodles transformed into great salads you can serve as unusual appetizers or filling main dishes.

Just imagine how Curried Stuffed Eggs will sparkle up the flavor and appearance of your next buffet. Easy to pick up, with that biting flavor unique to curry, these eggs will bring you many compliments and requests for the recipe. That long-time southern favorite — rice — receives special treatment in Rice Salad Vinaigrette ... and these are just two of the recipes women from throughout the Southland share with you in these pages.

Try one the next time you want to give a flavor lift to your entire menu. You'll be amazed at what they can do to transform the appearance of your whole meal!

141

Molded Cheddar Cheese Salad with Vegetables (below)

MOLDED CHEDDAR CHEESE SALAD WITH VEGETABLES

2 tsp. salt	1 c. shredded sharp American
1 tsp. dry mustard	cheese
2 tbsp. sugar	1/4 c. vinegar
Dash of hot sauce	1/4 c. pepper relish, well
1 env. unflavored gelatin	drained
2 eggs, slightly beaten	1 c. chopped celery
1 3/4 c. milk	1/4 c. chopped pimento

Mix the salt, mustard, sugar, hot sauce, gelatin, eggs and milk in top of a double boiler. Cook and stir over simmering water until the mixture coats a metal spoon. Do not have water touching top part of boiler. Remove from water at once. Add the cheese and stir until melted. Stir in the vinegar. Chill until mixture is consistency of unbeaten egg white, then fold in the pepper relish, celery and pimento. Pour into 8 individual molds or a 1 1/2-quart mold and chill until firm. Unmold and garnish with tomato wedges, sliced cucumbers and salad greens. Serve with French dressing or lemon mayonnaise. 8 servings.

CAMEMBERT MOUSSE

1 env. unflavored gelatin	1 tsp. Worcestershire sauce
2 1 1/3-oz. wedges camembert	1 egg, separated
cheese	1/2 c. heavy cream, whipped
3 1 1/4-oz. wedges Roquefort	Lettuce or watercress
cheese	

Soften the gelatin in 1/4 cup cold water. Place over hot water and stir until gelatin is dissolved. Blend the cheeses until smooth, then stir in the Worcestershire sauce, egg yolk and gelatin. Beat the egg white until stiff and fold into

142

cheese mixture. Fold in the whipped cream and place in 4 individual molds or a 3-cup mold. Refrigerate overnight. Unmold onto lettuce leaves or watercress.

Mrs. Harry S. Dennis, Jr., West Palm Beach, Florida

CHEESE-CARROT SALAD

1 3-oz. package orange gelatin	3 tbsp. grated bell pepper
1 c. hot water	2 tbsp. grated carrots
1 c. mayonnaise	1 carton creamed cottage
1 tbsp. grated onion	cheese

Dissolve the gelatin in hot water. Add the mayonnaise, onion, bell pepper and carrots and mix well. Stir in the cottage cheese and pour into a mold. Chill until firm. 8 servings.

Mrs. Dennis F. Jones, Decatur, Georgia

CLUB LUNCHEON SALAD

2 env. unflavored gelatin	1 c. mayonnaise
1 c. cold water	1 1/2 c. minced celery
1 can cream of mushroom soup	1/4 c. pickle relish
1 6-oz. package pimento	1 tsp. grated onion
cheese, crumbled	

Soften the gelatin in 1/2 cup water. Add remaining water to soup in a saucepan and bring to a boil. Add the gelatin and stir until dissolved. Add the cheese and stir until melted. Add mayonnaise and cool. Fold in remaining ingredients and pour into a 6-cup mold or 8 individual molds. Chill until firm. Unmold and garnish with salad greens, green pepper rings and carrot curls.

Mrs. L. J. Koons, St. Petersburg, Florida

COTTAGE CHEESE WITH WATERCRESS

3 c. cottage cheese	Lettuce
1 tsp. salt	Watercress
Dash of pepper	Tomato wedges
1/2 c. chopped radishes	Cucumber slices
1/4 c. finely chopped chives	Paprika
Mayonnaise	French dressing

Season the cottage cheese with salt and pepper. Add the radishes, chives and enough mayonnaise to moisten and mix well. Chill. Mound on lettuce and surround with watercress, tomato wedges and cucumber slices. Garnish with paprika and top with French dressing.

Bonnie Larsen, Columbia, South Carolina

GAINESVILLE CREAM CHEESE SALAD

1 tbsp. unflavored gelatin
1 No. 2 can crushed pineapple
1 pkg. lemon gelatin
Juice of 1 lemon
1/4 tsp. salt
1/4 c. chopped pimento

2 3-oz. packages cream cheese, softened
1/2 c. chopped nuts
1 stalk celery, chopped
6 marshmallows, quartered
1 c. whipped cream

Soften the unflavored gelatin in 1/4 cup cold water. Drain the pineapple and reserve juice. Add enough water to reserved juice to make 2 cups liquid and heat to boiling point. Add the lemon gelatin and unflavored gelatin and stir until dissolved. Add lemon juice and salt and chill until partially set. Mix the pineapple, cream cheese, pimento, nuts, celery and marshmallows and stir into gelatin mixture. Fold in the whipped cream and place in a mold. Chill until firm. 8 servings.

Mrs. Marie M. Mingledorff, Douglas, Georgia

GELATIN-CREAM SALAD

1 No. 2 1/2 can pineapple juice
2 3-oz. packages strawberry gelatin
1 8-oz. package cream cheese, softened

1 c. chopped pecans
1/2 c. chopped celery
1 can pimento strips, drained
1/2 pt. whipping cream, whipped

Pour the pineapple juice into a saucepan and heat to boiling point. Add the gelatin and stir until dissolved. Chill until thickened. Stir in the cream cheese, pecans, celery and pimento and fold in the whipped cream. Place in a mold and chill until firm.

Mrs. Ralph Worley, Canton, North Carolina

HORSERADISH COTTAGE SALAD

2 3-oz. packages lemon gelatin
1 No. 2 can crushed pineapple
1 lb. creamed cottage cheese

1 c. mayonnaise
1/2 c. walnut pieces
1/2 bottle horseradish

Dissolve the gelatin in 2 cups hot water and stir in remaining ingredients. Pour into a mold and refrigerate until firm. Serve on lettuce.

Mrs. Charles E. Shew, Tarpon Springs, Florida

ROYAL FROSTED FRUIT MOLD

1 c. milk
2 env. unflavored gelatin
2 12-oz. cartons cream-style cottage cheese
1/2 c. crumbled bleu cheese

1 6-oz. can frozen limeade concentrate, thawed
1/2 c. broken toasted pecans
6 drops of green food coloring
1 c. whipped cream

Pour the milk into a large saucepan and sprinkle gelatin over milk to soften. Place over low heat and stir until gelatin is dissolved. Remove from heat. Mix the cottage cheese and bleu cheese until well blended. Stir in the gelatin mixture, limeade concentrate, pecans and food coloring and fold in the whipped cream. Turn into 6-cup ring mold and chill until firm. Unmold on serving plate and garnish with frosted grapes and mint leaves. 10 servings.

Mrs. F. L. Love, Miami, Florida

MOLDED EGG SALAD

3 tbsp. unflavored gelatin	6 hard-cooked eggs
3/4 c. cold water	1/2 c. mayonnaise
3 c. boiling water	1/4 c. chopped parsley
1/4 c. sugar	1/2 c. chopped celery
3/4 c. lemon juice	1/2 c. chopped green olives

Soften the gelatin in cold water in a bowl. Add the boiling water, sugar and lemon juice and stir until the gelatin and sugar are dissolved. Cool. Cut the eggs in half and remove yolks. Mash the egg yolks and mix with 1/3 of the gelatin mixture. Stir in the mayonnaise and pour into a mold. Chill until firm, then sprinkle with chopped parsley. Chill remaining gelatin until thickened. Chop the egg whites and add to thickened gelatin. Add the celery and olives and mix well. Pour over congealed layer and chill until firm. Unmold onto a serving plate and garnish with hard-cooked egg slices and parsley sprigs. Top may be garnished with green peas and mushrooms, if desired.

Molded Egg Salad (above)

BOUNTIFUL EGG SALAD

13 hard-cooked eggs, chopped
1 c. diced celery
1 tsp. Worcestershire sauce
Dash of hot sauce
2 tbsp. grated onion
2 tbsp. chopped parsley
1/4 c. pickle relish

2 tbsp. lemon juice
1/4 c. chopped green pepper
1 env. unflavored gelatin
2 c. mayonnaise
3/4 tsp. salt
Pepper to taste

Combine the eggs, celery, sauces, onion, parsley, relish, lemon juice and green pepper. Soften the gelatin in 1/2 cup cold water and dissolve over boiling water. Beat in the mayonnaise. Add the egg mixture, salt and pepper and mix well. Place in a mold and chill until firm. 12 servings.

Mrs. H. H. Hankins, Rogers, Arkansas

DEVILED EGG-ASPIC SALAD

2 c. tomato juice
1 tsp. basil
1 tbsp. minced onion
1 tbsp. minced celery
1 tbsp. minced green pepper

1 3-oz. package lemon gelatin
2 tbsp. minced chives
1/2 tsp. salt
3 deviled eggs

Combine the tomato juice, basil, onion, celery and green pepper in a saucepan and bring to a boil. Remove from heat and strain. Add the gelatin, chives and salt and stir until gelatin is dissolved. Chill until thickened. Arrange eggs, cut side up, in a square baking dish and pour gelatin mixture over eggs. Chill until firm. Cut in squares and serve with salad dressing or sour cream dressing. 6 servings.

Charlotte R. Turner, Hendersonville, North Carolina

CURRIED-STUFFED EGGS

12 hard-cooked eggs
Mayonnaise
1 tsp. instant chicken bouillon
1/4 tsp. onion salt
1/4 tsp. white pepper

1 tsp. curry powder
1 c. minced cooked chicken (opt.)
Rolled anchovies
Olive slices
Capers

Cut eggs into halves lengthwise and remove yolks. Mash the egg yolks and add enough mayonnaise to moisten. Add the bouillon, onion salt, pepper, curry powder and chicken and mix thoroughly. Fill egg whites and top each half with an anchovy, olive slice and capers.

Mrs. A. C. Crowe, Ft. Walton, Florida

EGG AND PEANUT SALAD

6 hard-boiled eggs
2 tsp. vinegar
1 tsp. mustard

4 tbsp. mayonnaise
1/2 c. chopped peanuts

Cut the eggs in half and remove yolks. Mash the egg yolks and stir in the vinegar, mustard and mayonnaise. Blend in the peanuts and fill egg whites. Serve on lettuce leaves and garnish with celery curls and peanut halves.

Lorraine T. Carter, Raleigh, North Carolina

EGGS IN ASPIC

2 tbsp. unflavored gelatin	5 hard-boiled eggs, sliced thin
1/4 c. cold water	1 c. chopped sweet pickle
1 c. boiling water	1 c. chopped pecans
1/4 c. vinegar	1 c. mayonnaise
1 c. cooked sm. green peas	

Soften the gelatin in cold water. Add boiling water and stir until dissolved. Cool. Add the vinegar, peas, eggs, pickle, pecans and mayonnaise and mix well. Pour into lightly oiled mold and chill until firm. Serve on lettuce and garnish with mayonnaise and stuffed olives. 8 servings.

Mrs. W. W. Harman, Birmingham, Alabama

CALIFORNIA AVOCADO BALL SALAD

1 lge. head romaine	4 diced hard-cooked eggs
1 lge. head curly endive	5 slices crisp bacon, crumbled
1 lge. head leaf lettuce	3 or 4 lge. avocados
1 bunch spinach	Bottled French dressing

Tear the romaine, endive, lettuce and spinach in small pieces and place in a salad bowl. Add the eggs and bacon and toss lightly. Cut balls from the avocados with a large melon ball scoop and place on salad. Drizzle with French dressing.

California Avocado Ball Salad (above)

EGG-CROWNED SUPPER MOLD

4 hard-cooked eggs	1 tsp. sugar
1 env. unflavored gelatin	1/2 tsp. celery salt
1 3/4 c. chicken broth	2 1/2 c. diced cooked potatoes
3 tbsp. prepared mustard	2 c. diced baked ham
3 tbsp. sweet pickle relish	Pepper to taste
3 tbsp. diced green pepper	1/2 c. mayonnaise
2 tbsp. instant minced onion	

Cut the eggs in half crosswise, then cut each piece in half. Soften the gelatin in 1/4 cup chicken broth. Heat remaining broth in a saucepan. Add gelatin mixture and stir until dissolved. Place a 6-cup ring mold in a pan of ice. Pour 2 to 3 tablespoons gelatin mixture into the mold and rotate to coat bottom of mold. Stand egg pieces on end in a circle on congealed gelatin and spoon 6 tablespoons gelatin mixture around egg pieces. Chill until firm. Combine the mustard, pickle relish, green pepper, onion, sugar and celery salt and stir in remaining gelatin mixture. Add the potatoes, ham, any remaining pieces of egg and pepper and mix well. Chill until thickened and fold in mayonnaise. Spoon over eggs in mold and chill until firm. Serve on lettuce and garnish with stuffed olives. 6 servings.

Mrs. B. R. Rawlings, Shreveport, Louisiana

EGG SALAD OVER TOMATO SLICES

8 hard-cooked eggs, chopped	Salt and pepper to taste
1 c. diced celery	6 thick tomato slices
1/4 c. salad dressing	Salad greens
1 tsp. Worcestershire sauce	Paprika
1 tbsp. lemon juice	Celery curls
1 tsp. grated onion	

Combine the eggs, celery, salad dressing, Worcestershire sauce, lemon juice, onion, salt and pepper. Press into 6 individual molds and chill. Unmold on tomato slices placed on salad greens and sprinkle with paprika. Garnish with celery curls.

Zelda Leigh Powell, Mandeville, Louisiana

HEART OF GOLD SALAD

8 hard-boiled eggs	1/2 tsp. salt
1 pkg. lemon gelatin	2 tsp. grated onion
1 c. boiling water	3/4 c. diced celery
3/4 c. beet juice	1 c. diced cooked beets
3 tbsp. vinegar	

Arrange the eggs in a square baking dish. Dissolve the gelatin in boiling water in a bowl. Stir in the beet juice, vinegar, salt and onion and chill until slightly thickened. Fold in the celery and beets and pour over the eggs. Chill until firm. Cut into squares and serve on lettuce.

Kathryn S. Johnson, St. Petersburg, Florida

LETTUCE-EGG SALAD

1 head lettuce	Salt and pepper to taste
1 sm. onion, chopped fine	Mayonnaise
2 hard-cooked eggs, chopped	4 slices fried bacon, crumbled

Break the lettuce into small pieces and place in a bowl. Add the onion, eggs, salt, pepper and enough mayonnaise to moisten and mix well. Top with bacon and serve immediately. 6 servings.

Beth White, Goliad, Texas

ST. LOUIS SALAD

1 clove of garlic, sliced	1 tbsp. light corn syrup
1 stalk celery, sliced	3 eggs
1/2 med. onion, sliced	1 pt. corn oil
1 2-oz. can anchovy fillets	1 lge. head western iceberg
2 tbsp. mustard with horseradish	lettuce
1 tbsp. lemon juice	2 hard-boiled eggs, finely
1 tsp. cracked pepper	chopped
1 tsp. monosodium glutamate	1/2 c. crisp croutons

Place the garlic, celery and onion in a blender container. Add the anchovy fillets, mustard, lemon juice, pepper, monosodium glutamate and corn syrup and blend until mixed. Add eggs and blend for several seconds. Add the corn oil, 1/2 cup at a time, blending after each addition. Tear the lettuce into bite-sized pieces into a salad bowl. Place the hard-boiled eggs in center of lettuce and sprinkle lettuce with croutons. Toss with 1/4 to 1/2 cup dressing or enough to coat ingredients. Store remaining dressing in refrigerator for later use.

St. Louis Salad (above)

149

INDIAN SALAD

1 No. 2 can hominy	2 tbsp. coarsely grated carrot
3 tbsp. catsup	3 tbsp. mayonnaise
1 tbsp. chopped onion	1 c. cottage cheese
1 tbsp. chopped pimento	Salt to taste
2 tbsp. chopped dill pickle	

Simmer the hominy in a saucepan for 10 minutes, then drain. Place in a bowl. Add the catsup, onion and pimento and mix. Cool. Stir in remaining ingredients and chill.

Mrs. Henry J. Pohl, Hallettsville, Texas

RICE-BEAN SALAD

1 1-lb. can kidney beans	1/4 c. chopped green pepper
1 c. cooked rice	1/2 tsp. salt
2 hard-cooked eggs, chopped	1/4 tsp. pepper
1/2 c. chopped sweet pickles	1/3 c. mayonnaise
1/4 c. chopped onion	Crisp lettuce
1/4 c. chopped celery	

Drain the kidney beans and place in a bowl. Stir in remaining ingredients except lettuce and chill. Serve on lettuce. 6-8 servings.

Mrs. James E. Mast, Amelia, Virginia

RICE SALAD VINAIGRETTE

3 tbsp. olive oil	1/4 c. chopped onion
1 tbsp. wine vinegar	1/4 c. diced celery
1 tsp. salt	1/4 c. seeded diced cucumber
1/2 tsp. pepper	1/4 c. diced green pepper
2 c. cooked rice	

Mix the olive oil, vinegar, salt and pepper in a bowl. Add the rice, onion, celery, cucumber and green pepper and mix well. Place in a salad bowl and garnish with parsley.

Mrs. Helen G. Morris, Prescott, Arkansas

STUFFED TOMATO SALAD

6 lge. tomatoes	1 tsp. onion juice
1 1/2 c. cooked brown rice	1 tbsp. basil
2 tbsp. chopped celery	Salad dressing

Cut off tops of tomatoes and scoop out centers. Mix the rice with remaining ingredients, adding enough salad dressing to moisten, and place in tomatoes. Serve on lettuce or watercress with cottage cheese dressing, if desired.

Mrs. Hazel Tilghman, Kinston, North Carolina

RICE SLAW

1/4 c. grated carrots	1 med. tomato, chopped
1/4 c. diced green pepper	1/4 c. diced pickles
1 hard-cooked egg, finely	2 c. cooked rice
chopped	3/4 c. salad dressing
1 c. diced celery	Salt to taste

Combine all ingredients in a bowl and mix lightly. Chill. One small jar pimentos, drained and chopped, may be substituted for tomato. 6 servings.

Mrs. G. D. Bell, Des Arc, Arkansas

SURFSIDE SALAD

2 2/3 c. water	1 med. green pepper, chopped
1 2-oz. package creamy French	2 pimentos, cut in sm. pieces
salad dressing mix	1 c. mayonnaise
1 tbsp. instant minced onion	3 tbsp. lemon juice
2 2/3 c. packaged precooked rice	3 tbsp. vinegar
1 1/2 c. diagonally sliced celery	

Mix the water, salad dressing mix and onion in a saucepan and bring to a boil. Stir in the rice and cover. Remove from heat and let stand for 5 minutes. Add the celery, green pepper and pimentos and mix lightly. Place the mayonnaise in a bowl and stir in the lemon juice and vinegar gradually. Add to rice mixture and mix lightly until well blended. Chill. Serve with salad greens. 8 servings.

Surfside Salad (above)

TROPICAL RICE SALAD

1 c. rice	1 c. chopped dates
2 c. orange juice	1/2 c. toasted slivered almonds
1/4 tsp. salt	6 thin honeydew melon slices
1 tsp. grated lemon rind	6 thin cantaloupe slices
1 tbsp. lemon juice	

Combine the rice, orange juice and salt in a 3-quart saucepan and bring to a boil. Stir well and cover tightly. Reduce heat and simmer for about 20 minutes. Chill. Mix in the lemon rind and juice, dates and almonds. Place 1 slice honeydew melon on each of 6 individual salad plates. Place a cantaloupe slice on each honeydew melon slice and fill center with the rice mixture.

Minted Sour Cream Dressing

1 c. sour cream	1 tsp. lemon juice
1 tbsp. finely chopped mint	Dash of salt
2 tsp. sugar	

Mix the sour cream, mint, sugar, lemon juice and salt in a bowl and chill. Serve with the salad.

Mrs. Gloria Elick, Hammond, Louisiana

TABOULI SALAD

1 c. cracked wheat seed	4 tomatoes, finely chopped
1/2 c. olive oil	2 cucumbers, finely chopped
Juice of 3 lemons	1 lge. onion, chopped
1 tsp. salt	Chopped parsley

Soak the wheat seed in enough warm water to cover for about 30 minutes, then drain. Mix in the olive oil, lemon juice and salt. Mix the tomatoes, cucumbers and onion in a bowl and pour the oil mixture over top. Refrigerate for several hours. Toss lightly and garnish with parsley.

Mrs. Hoyal Sloan, Pryor, Oklahoma

FRUITED RICE SALAD

1/2 c. diced celery	1 c. water
1/4 c. minced onion	1/3 c. raisins or
2 tbsp. butter or margarine	currants (opt.)
2 tsp. grated orange peel	1 c. rice
1/2 tsp. poultry seasoning	6 fluted orange shells
1 c. orange juice	

Saute the celery and onion in butter in a saucepan until tender. Add remaining ingredients except orange shells and bring to a boil. Stir well. Reduce heat and cover. Simmer for about 25 minutes or until rice is tender and liquid is absorbed. Cool, then chill. Serve in orange shells. 6 servings.

ELBOW SALAD

3 c. cooked elbow macaroni	Salt
2 hard-cooked eggs, sliced	1/2 c. sugar
6 slices fried bacon, crumbled	1 tbsp. flour
1/2 c. chopped celery	1/8 tsp. pepper
1/4 c. chopped parsley	1/2 c. vinegar
1/4 c. chopped green pepper	1/2 c. water
1/2 c. sliced radishes	2 eggs, beaten
2 tbsp. chopped onion	1 tsp. prepared mustard

Place the macaroni in a bowl. Add the hard-cooked eggs, bacon, celery, parsley, green pepper, radishes, onion and salt to taste and toss well. Chill. Mix the sugar, 1 teaspoon salt, flour and pepper in top of a double boiler. Add remaining ingredients and cook over boiling water until thick, stirring constantly. Cool, then add to macaroni mixture. Toss well and garnish with green pepper rings and additional radish slices.

Alberta Cromer, Townville, South Carolina

SUMMER MACARONI SALAD

1 7-oz. package ring macaroni	1/2 c. minced onion
1 10-oz. package frozen peas	1/2 c. mayonnaise
1 c. cubed Cheddar cheese	Salt and pepper to taste
1 c. sliced gherkins	

Cook the macaroni according to package directions and drain. Rinse with cold water and drain again. Cook the peas according to package directions and drain. Cool. Place in a bowl and stir in the macaroni and remaining ingredients. Chill. Serve in lettuce cups, if desired. 6 servings.

Nelda Lowry, Caddo Mills, Texas

Fruited Rice Salad (page 152)

MACARONI-TUNA LUNCH BOX SALAD

Salt
3 qt. boiling water
2 c. elbow macaroni
2 6 1/2 to 7-oz. cans tuna, drained
1/2 c. slivered green pepper
1/2 c. mayonnaise

1 8 3/4-oz. can pineapple tidbits, drained
1/4 c. toasted slivered almonds
1/4 tsp. onion salt
1/4 tsp. chervil
1/8 tsp. white pepper
3 tbsp. lemon juice

Add 1 tablespoon salt to boiling water and add macaroni gradually so that water continues to boil. Cook, stirring occasionally, until tender, then drain in a colander. Rinse with cold water and drain again. Combine 1/4 teaspoon salt and remaining ingredients with macaroni in a large bowl and toss. Chill. Pack in wide-mouth vacuum bottle for lunch box.

Photograph for this recipe on page 140.

MENCHI'S MACARONI SALAD

1/2 8-oz. package elbow macaroni
1/2 c. chopped cucumber
1/2 c. chopped green pepper
1/2 c. chopped onion
1/2 c. diced avocado
1 lge. tomato, diced

3 hard-boiled eggs, chopped
1 1/2 tsp. salt
Dash of pepper
1/4 c. French dressing
1 c. salad dressing
1 pkg. sour cream sauce mix

Cook the macaroni according to package directions, then blanch and drain. Place in a bowl. Add remaining ingredients in order listed and mix carefully but well. Chill. 8 servings.

Mrs. Louise W. Peck, Fayetteville, Tennessee

PICNIC NOODLE SALAD

Salt
3 qt. boiling water
8 oz. medium egg noodles
1 1/2 c. mayonnaise
1 tsp. caraway seed
1/8 tsp. pepper

1 1-lb. can ham, cubed
1/2 lb. Swiss cheese, cubed
1/2 c. sliced olives
1/2 c. chopped celery
Crisp chicory

Add 1 tablespoon salt to boiling water and add the noodles gradually so that water continues to boil. Cook, stirring occasionally, until tender, then drain in a colander. Rinse with cold water and drain again. Combine the mayonnaise, caraway seed, 1 teaspoon salt and pepper in a large bowl. Add the noodles, ham, cheese, olives and celery and toss well. Chill. Garnish with chicory just before serving. 6 servings.

Oceale Bishop, Mt. Airy, North Carolina

SPAGHETTI SALAD

1 9-oz. package spaghetti
3 hard-cooked eggs, chopped

2 stalks celery, chopped
2 sweet pickles, chopped

2 green onions, chopped
3 tbsp. grated Parmesan cheese
1 tsp. chopped parsley
1 c. mayonnaise

1 tsp. salt
Dash of pepper
1 tbsp. vinegar
1 tsp. Worcestershire sauce

Break the spaghetti into short lengths and cook in boiling, salted water until tender. Drain and cool. Place in a bowl. Add the eggs, celery, pickles, onions, cheese and parsley and mix. Combine the mayonnaise, salt, pepper, vinegar and Worcestershire sauce. Add to spaghetti mixture and mix thoroughly. Chill. 6-8 servings.

Mrs. Dean Fuller, Frederick, Maryland

MACARONI AND BEEF BONUS SALAD

2 1/2 tsp. salt
1 1/2 qt. boiling water
2 c. shell or elbow macaroni
2 c. cubed cooked beef or lamb
1/2 c. sliced sweet gherkins
1 c. diced celery
1/3 c. coarsely chopped red or
    sweet onion

1 c. grated sharp natural
    Cheddar cheese
1 c. salad dressing or
    mayonnaise
1 tbsp. red wine vinegar
1 tsp. prepared mustard
1/4 tsp. pepper
Dash of cayenne pepper

Add 1 1/2 teaspoons salt to boiling water and add the macaroni gradually so that water continues to boil. Cook, stirring occasionally, until tender, then drain in a colander. Rinse in cold water and drain again. Combine the beef, macaroni, gherkins, celery, onion and cheese. Mix the salad dressing, vinegar, mustard, remaining salt, pepper and cayenne pepper and add to beef mixture. Toss lightly and chill. Serve on lettuce and garnish with additional cheese, if desired. 6 servings.

Macaroni and Beef Bonus Salad (above)

elegant frozen salads

Using the freezer of their refrigerators . . . and the plenitude of fresh fruits and vegetables available year-round in the Southland, creative homemakers throughout this region have developed many diverse frozen salads.

These are the salads they serve when hot weather has jaded appetites . . . when the traditional roast meat and potato main dish needs some contrast . . . or when they want to transform an ordinary supper into a special meal. Because they expect their frozen salads to play such demanding roles in menu planning, they have taken special care to develop recipes to please every palate.

Fruit flavors harmonize when you serve French Fruit Salad — a dish elegant enough to double as a centerpiece or as a party dessert. And for unusual salad service, try Frozen Salad in Orange Shells. They'll be a real conversation piece at your next dinner party! Another party-perfect salad is Rainbow Frozen Fruit Salad, a rich blend of eye-appealing colors and palate-pleasing flavors.

These three recipes are just the beginning of the wonderful dishes awaiting you in this section. You'll find a frozen salad for every occasion and for every taste when you choose one of these recipes from the kitchens of southern women. Best of all, these are home-tested, family-proven recipes which have brought compliments and praise to the women who invite you to serve a frozen salad — now!

157

FROZEN CRANBERRY SALAD

1 1-lb. can jellied cranberry sauce	1/4 c. mayonnaise
3 tbsp. lemon juice	1/2 c. confectioners' sugar
1 c. heavy cream, whipped	1 c. chopped nuts

Crush the cranberry sauce with a fork and add the lemon juice. Pour into paper cups or refrigerator tray. Combine the remaining ingredients and spread over the cranberry mixture. Freeze until firm. Unmold on lettuce and garnish with whole nuts. 8 servings.

Mrs. J. T. Teas, Haleyville, Alabama

FROZEN PEAR AND CREAM CHEESE SALAD

1 1-lb. can pears	6 tbsp. French dressing
2 3-oz. packages cream cheese	

Drain the juice from the pears and reserve the juice. Cut the pears into thin lengthwise slices. Mash the cream cheese and add the reserved pear juice and French dressing. Beat with electric mixer until smooth. Arrange pear slices in refrigerator tray and pour the cheese mixture over pears. Freeze until firm enough to slice into squares. Serve on salad greens and garnish with mayonnaise or additional French dressing.

Mrs. E. N. Cross, Johnson City, Tennessee

ROSY PINK SALADS

1 c. whipping cream	1 1-lb. can whole cranberry sauce
1/4 c. sugar	1/2 6-oz. can frozen orange
Dash of salt	juice concentrate, thawed
2 tbsp. mayonnaise	1 c. miniature marshmallows

Combine cream, sugar and salt and whip until soft peaks form. Stir in the mayonnaise and mix well. Fold in the cranberry sauce, orange concentrate and marshmallows. Line muffin tins with paper baking cups and fill with cranberry mixture. Freeze until firm. Remove to refrigerator for about 10 minutes before serving time. Peel off paper cups and unmold onto salad greens. Garnish with a pickled peach, a spiced crab apple or orange sections.

Mrs. W. H. Ross, Morton, Mississippi

APPLE-ORANGE FROST

1 No. 2 can applesauce	3 tbsp. sugar
1 sm. can orange juice	3 egg whites, stiffly beaten
2 or 3 tbsp. lemon juice	

Combine the applesauce, orange juice, lemon juice and sugar, then fold in the egg whites. Pour into a freezing tray and freeze until firm. Salad will keep from 2 to 4 weeks in freezer.

Mrs. B. A. Jones, San Antonio, Texas

CHERRY-PINEAPPLE SALAD

2 c. pineapple juice
2 3-oz. packages lemon gelatin
1 8-oz. package cream cheese,
  softened
1 4-oz. can red cherries,
  drained

1 4-oz. can green cherries,
  drained
1 c. broken pecans
8 slices pineapple, cubed
1 pt. heavy cream, whipped

Bring the pineapple juice to a boil and add the gelatin, then stir until the gelatin is dissolved. Chill until thickened. Add the cream cheese, cherries, pecans and pineapple. Fold in the whipped cream and turn into refrigerator trays. Freeze overnight. Serve on lettuce. 8 servings.

Mrs. S. K. Engel, Yuma, Arizona

FROZEN PEACH SALAD

1 1-lb. 13-oz. can cling peach
  slices
1 3-oz. package lemon gelatin
2 tbsp. lemon juice
1/8 tsp. salt

1/3 c. salad dressing
2/3 c. whipping cream, whipped
1 10-oz. package frozen sliced
  strawberries, slightly thawed

Drain the peaches and reserve 1 cup syrup. Reserve 6 peach slices for garnish and dice remaining peaches. Pour reserved syrup into a saucepan and bring to boiling point. Add the gelatin and stir until dissolved. Stir in the lemon juice and salt. Blend the salad dressing with half the gelatin mixture and chill until slightly thickened. Fold in the diced peaches and half the whipped cream. Turn into an 11 x 4 x 1 1/2-inch refrigerator tray or 9 x 5 x 2 3/4-inch loaf pan and freeze. Add the strawberries to remaining gelatin and chill until slightly thickened. Fold in remaining whipped cream and place on peach layer in refrigerator tray. Freeze until firm. Unmold and garnish with reserved peach slices and, if desired, with whole strawberries and salad greens. 8-10 servings.

Frozen Peach Salad (above)

FROZEN PEACH AND PECAN SALAD

8 peach halves
1 8-oz. package cream cheese
1 c. mayonnaise

1 c. chopped pecans
1 c. heavy cream, whipped

Arrange the peach halves, hollow side up, in a refrigerator tray. Combine the cream cheese and mayonnaise and blend well. Fold in the pecans and whipped cream. Pour over the peach halves. Freeze for 3 to 4 hours. Cut into 8 pieces. Serve on crisp salad greens.

Priscilla Childers, Cullman, Alabama

THREE-TIERED DESSERT SALAD

1 qt. pistachio ice cream
1 c. chopped cherries
1 1/2 pt. strawberry ice cream
1 c. mashed strawberries

1 pt. vanilla ice cream
1 sm. can crushed pineapple,
 drained
Dark corn syrup

Mix the pistachio ice cream and cherries and pack into large pan of wedding cake tier pan set. Freeze until firm. Mix the strawberry ice cream and strawberries and pack into medium pan. Freeze until firm. Mix the vanilla ice cream and pineapple and pack into small pan. Freeze until firm. Unmold the ice creams and stack on a serving plate. Serve with a topping of dark corn syrup.

Photograph for this recipe on page 156.

BANANA SALAD

4 bananas, mashed
2 tbsp. lemon juice
1/2 c. sugar
1/4 c. mayonnaise

1/2 c. chopped maraschino
 cherries
1/2 c. chopped walnuts
3/4 c. heavy cream, whipped

Blend the bananas with the lemon juice, sugar, mayonnaise, cherries and walnuts. Fold in the whipped cream. Place in a freezing tray. Freeze. Serve on lettuce leaves and garnish with walnuts. 8 servings.

Mrs. G. C. Carter, Chattanooga, Tennessee

BERRY-ICE CREAM SALAD

1 qt. vanilla ice cream
1/2 c. mayonnaise
1 c. drained crushed pineapple

1 c. drained blueberries
2 c. raspberries or strawberries

Soften the ice cream and blend in the mayonnaise quickly. Add the fruits and mix. Pour into freezer tray and freeze for 2 to 3 hours or until firm.

Mrs. J. K. Moore, Jackson, Mississippi

BANANA-SOUR CREAM JUBILEE

2 c. sour cream	4 tbsp. chopped maraschino
3/4 c. sugar	cherries
2 tbsp. lemon juice	1/2 c. miniature marshmallows
1 sm. can crushed pineapple	2 bananas, mashed
Salt to taste (opt.)	1/2 c. chopped nuts

Combine all the ingredients and mix well. Pour into paper baking cups and freeze. Serve on lettuce. Garnish with cherries, nuts, lemon twists, mint leaves or orange slices.

Mrs. L. G. Crane, Biloxi, Mississippi

FROZEN CITRUS SALAD

1 c. orange pieces	1/2 c. shredded coconut
1 c. miniature marshmallows	1 3-oz. package cream cheese
1/4 c. sliced red or green	1/4 c. mayonnaise
maraschino cherries	1/4 tsp. salt

Mix the orange pieces, marshmallows, cherries and coconut in a bowl. Beat the cream cheese until soft. Add the mayonnaise and salt and mix well. Blend with the fruit mixture. Pour into refrigerator tray and freeze. Serve on lettuce. 6-8 servings.

Frozen Citrus Salad (above)

FRENCH FRUIT SALAD

1 tbsp. lemon juice	1/3 c. French dressing
2 bananas, diced	1 c. whipped cream
3/4 c. diced pineapple	1/2 c. mayonnaise
12 red maraschino cherries,	1/8 tsp. salt
chopped	2 tbsp. confectioners' sugar

Pour the lemon juice over the bananas and add pineapple, cherries and French dressing. Chill for 2 hours, then drain. Fold the whipped cream into the mayonnaise, then add the salt and sugar. Fold in the fruit mixture. Spoon in mold and freeze.

Mrs. Ray Sartor, Ripley, Mississippi

FROZEN FRUIT-HONEY SALAD

2 tbsp. sugar	1 c. sliced bananas
1 tbsp. flour	1/3 c. diced orange slices
1/2 c. honey	1/4 c. pitted and quartered
1 egg	Bing cherries
1/3 c. lemon juice	1 c. whipped cream
2 c. drained fruit cocktail	

Combine the sugar, flour and honey. Bring to a boil and cook for 1 minute, stirring constantly. Beat the egg and add the lemon juice gradually. Add a small amount of honey mixture to egg and mix well. Return to honey mixture and bring to a boil, stirring constantly. Remove from heat and cool. Combine the fruits and add to the honey mixture. Fold in the whipped cream. Freeze.

Mrs. B. K. Norris, Lexington, Kentucky

FROSTY HALF AND HALF SALAD

1 No. 2 1/2 can peach halves	2 tbsp. cream
1 No. 2 1/2 can pear halves	1/4 tsp. paprika
2 3-oz. packages cream cheese,	Dash of salt
softened	1/2 c. chopped pecans

Drain the peach and pear halves. Combine the cream cheese, cream, paprika, salt and pecans and mix well. Fill the centers of peach halves. Top each peach half with a pear half and press together. Wrap separately in waxed paper and place in refrigerator trays. Freeze until slightly firm.

Edna Mae Basden, Rienzi, Mississippi

FROZEN PEACH-PINEAPPLE SALAD

1 No. 2 can crushed pineapple	1/4 c. mayonnaise
1 3-oz. package cream cheese,	1 c. miniature marshmallows
softened	1/2 c. chopped pecans

1 c. diced drained peaches
1/4 c. chopped maraschino
cherries

1 c. diced bananas
1 c. heavy cream, whipped

Drain the pineapple. Blend the cream cheese and mayonnaise together and add the pineapple, marshmallows, pecans, peaches, cherries and bananas. Mix well. Fold the whipped cream into the fruit mixture, then spoon into two 1 1/2-pint waxed paper freezer cartons. Place in freezer and freeze until firm. Slice to serve. Will keep for several months in freezer.

Mrs. C. P. Todd, Enid, Oklahoma

FROZEN PINK PEARL

1 1-lb. can apricot halves
1 1-lb. can cling peach
slices
1 3-oz. package strawberry
gelatin
2 tbsp. lemon juice

1 8-oz. package cream cheese,
softened
1/2 c. mayonnaise
1 1/2 c. miniature marshmallows
1/2 c. sliced maraschino cherries
1/2 c. whipping cream, whipped

Drain the apricots and peaches and reserve 1 1/4 cups juice. Cut into small pieces. Dissolve the gelatin in 1 cup hot water and add the reserved juice and lemon juice. Chill until thickened. Blend the cream cheese and mayonnaise together until smooth, then stir in the gelatin. Place bowl in larger bowl of ice and chill until thickened, stirring frequently. Fold the apricots, peaches, marshmallows and cherries into gelatin, then fold in the whipped cream carefully. Spoon into an 8-cup mold. Freeze for at least 6 hours or overnight. Unmold by quickly dipping mold in pan of hot water and inverting on serving plate. Garnish with watercress. 10-12 servings.

Mrs. F. R. DeBray, Mobile, Alabama

GOLDEN PEACH FREEZE

1 10-oz. package frozen sliced
peaches
2 3-oz. packages cream cheese
1 c. heavy cream
1/3 c. mayonnaise
2 tbsp. lemon juice

1 c. miniature marshmallows
1 1-lb. 15-oz. can crushed
pineapple, drained
Few drops of yellow food
coloring

Thaw and drain peaches. Beat the cream cheese until smooth, then add the cream slowly beating constantly until thick and fluffy. Fold in remaining ingredients and pour into muffin pans lined with cupcake papers. Garnish with nuts and maraschino cherries. Freeze until firm. Remove from pans and place in plastic bags, then return to freezer. Remove from freezer in the quantity desired and remove paper cups. Serve on crisp greens. 18 servings.

Mrs. Richard Claycomb, Guston, Kentucky

Frozen Fruit Salad (below)

FROZEN FRUIT SALAD

2 tbsp. sugar	1 11-oz. can mandarin
1 tbsp. flour	oranges
1/2 c. honey	1 c. sliced dried figs
1/4 c. lemon juice	1/2 c. flaked coconut
1 egg, beaten	1 c. heavy cream, whipped

Combine the sugar, flour and honey in a saucepan and bring to a boil. Mix the lemon juice and egg, then stir into honey mixture. Heat to boiling point, stirring constantly. Remove from heat and cool. Drain the oranges and add to honey mixture. Stir in the figs and coconut. Fold in the whipped cream. Pour into refrigerator tray or individual molds and freeze until firm. 8 servings.

FROZEN PRUNE SALAD

1 c. chopped cooked prunes	1 3-oz. package cream cheese,
1/2 c. drained crushed pineapple	softened
1/2 c. halved maraschino cherries	1/4 c. mayonnaise
1 banana	1 c. heavy cream
1 tbsp. lemon juice	

Combine the prunes, pineapple and cherries. Mash the banana and mix with the lemon juice. Blend the cream cheese, banana and mayonnaise together. Whip the cream until soft peaks form, then fold in fruit mixtures. Turn into refrigerator tray and freeze until almost firm. Serve on salad greens. 6-8 servings.

Mrs. M. O. Prentiss, Raleigh, North Carolina

FROZEN SALAD IN ORANGE SHELLS

4 oranges
2 3-oz. packages cream cheese,
   softened
1/4 c. mayonnaise
1 tbsp. vinegar

1/4 tsp. mustard
1 1/2 c. diced fresh fruit
1/4 c. slivered almonds
1/2 c. heavy cream, whipped

Cut the oranges into halves and scoop out centers, reserving one-half of the orange pulp. Dice reserved orange pulp. Blend the cream cheese with mayonnaise, vinegar and mustard, then add the orange pulp, diced fruit and almonds. Fold in the whipped cream and heap into the orange shells. Freeze until firm. Let shells stand at room temperature for 10 minutes before serving. 8 servings.

Mrs. C. R. Boyd, New Orleans, Louisiana

GINGER-FRUIT FREEZE

1 3-oz. package cream cheese
3 tbsp. mayonnaise
1 tbsp. lemon juice
1/4 tsp. salt
1/2 c. chopped preserved kumquats
1/2 c. chopped dates

1/4 c. quartered maraschino cherries
1 9-oz. can crushed pineapple,
   drained
2 tbsp. minced candied ginger
1 c. heavy cream, whipped
1/4 c. toasted slivered almonds

Soften the cream cheese and blend in the mayonnaise, lemon juice and salt. Stir in the fruits and ginger, then fold in the whipped cream. Pour into a 1-quart freezer tray and sprinkle with the almonds. Freeze until firm. 6-8 servings.

Mrs. S. C. Jordan, Norfolk, Virginia

GINGER ALE SALAD

1 1/2 tsp. unflavored gelatin
2 tbsp. orange juice
1 tbsp. lemon juice
2 tbsp. sugar
1/2 c. ginger ale
1/4 c. drained crushed pineapple

1/3 c. diced canned pears
1/4 c. halved strawberries
1/3 c. chopped nuts (opt.)
1/3 c. mayonnaise
1/2 c. heavy cream, whipped

Soften the gelatin in orange juice for 5 minutes, then add the lemon juice. Place over boiling water and stir until gelatin is dissolved. Add sugar and ginger ale and stir until sugar is dissolved. Add the fruits and nuts and mix thoroughly. Fold in the mayonnaise and whipped cream. Pour into a small freezing tray and freeze until firm. 6 servings.

Mrs. S. A. Haynes, Monroe, Louisiana

GRACE'S ROYAL SALAD

1 1-lb. can apricot halves	1/4 tsp. salt
1 8-oz. package cream cheese, softened	1 1/2 c. pitted halved Bing cherries
1 c. sour cream	2 c. miniature marshmallows
1/4 c. sugar	Few drops of red food coloring

Drain and slice the apricots. Beat the cream cheese until fluffy, then stir in the sour cream, sugar and salt. Add the remaining ingredients and mix well. Pour into an 8 1/2 x 4 1/2 x 2 1/2-inch loaf pan. Freeze for 6 hours or overnight. Let stand at room temperature for several minutes, then remove from pan. Slice and serve on crisp greens. Garnish with cherries and peach slices. 8 servings.

Mrs. Raymond Williams, Morrison, Tennessee

GRAPEFRUIT-AVOCADO SALAD

1 8-oz. package cream cheese, softened	1 grapefruit, sectioned
1 c. sour cream	1 avocado, diced
1/4 tsp. salt	1 c. halved seedless white grapes
1/2 c. sugar	1/2 c. broken pecans

Blend the cream cheese and sour cream together and add the salt and sugar. Stir until well blended. Add grapefruit sections, avocado, grapes and pecans. Pour into a 9 x 5-inch loaf pan and freeze until firm. Slice and serve on salad greens with French dressing. 6-8 servings.

Mrs. D. S. Callahan, Bradenton, Florida

PINEAPPLE SALAD

2 sm. packages cream cheese	1 lb. marshmallows
1 c. salad dressing	1 c. chopped pecans
1 can crushed pineapple	1 c. whipping cream, whipped
2 sm. jars maraschino cherries	

Combine cream cheese and salad dressing and whip until smooth. Add the pineapple, cherries, marshmallows and pecans and blend. Place in freezing trays, then spread whipped cream over top. Place in freezer and freeze until firm. Slice to serve.

Mrs. Leonard Gibbs, Sonora, Texas

RAINBOW FROZEN FRUIT SALAD

22 marshmallows	3 bananas, sliced
1 c. canned crushed pineapple	1 c. diced peaches
1/2 c. mayonnaise	1 c. raspberries
1/2 pt. heavy cream, whipped	

Combine 16 marshmallows and pineapple in a saucepan. Cook over low heat, stirring constantly, until marshmallows are melted. Cool until slightly thickened. Quarter remaining marshmallows and add with the mayonnaise, whipped cream, and fruits. Pour into trays and freeze without stirring. Slice and serve on crisp lettuce. 8 servings.

Mrs. J. H. Martin, Louisville, Kentucky

RARE DELIGHT

1/2 cantaloupe, diced	1 c. halved white grapes
4 red plums, diced	1 can frozen orange juice
1 c. halved fresh red cherries	

Combine the fruits and mix lightly. Place in ice cube tray. Combine orange juice with 1 1/2 cans water and pour over fruit. Freeze until mushy. Serve on lettuce and garnish with mayonnaise. 4 servings.

Mrs. G. D. Kelley, Newport, Kentucky

PINEAPPLE-BLUEBERRY SALAD FREEZE

1 1-lb. 4 1/2-oz. can crushed pineapple	1 c. sour cream
2 1/2 c. miniature marshmallows	2/3 c. mayonnaise
1/4 tsp. salt	3/4 c. blueberries
	3 1/2 tbsp. lemon juice

Combine the undrained pineapple, marshmallows and salt in a saucepan and stir over low heat until marshmallows are melted. Cool. Stir in the sour cream and mayonnaise. Place the blueberries and lemon juice in blender container and blend until smooth. Stir into the pineapple mixture. Turn into an 8 1/2-inch ring mold and freeze until firm. Remove from freezer to refrigerator 20 to 30 minutes before serving. Unmold and slice to serve. 8 servings.

Pineapple-Blueberry Salad Freeze (above)

PINK ARCTIC FREEZE

2 3-oz. packages cream cheese
2 tbsp. mayonnaise
3 tbsp. sugar
1 1-lb. can whole cranberry
   sauce

1 9-oz. can crushed pineapple,
   drained
1/2 c. chopped walnuts or pecans
1 c. heavy cream, whipped

Blend cream cheese, mayonnaise and sugar together. Add cranberry sauce, pineapple and walnuts and mix thoroughly. Fold in the whipped cream. Pour into an 8 1/2 x 4 1/2 x 2 1/2-inch loaf pan and freeze for 6 hours or overnight. Let stand at room temperature for 15 minutes before serving, then slice and serve on lettuce. 8-10 servings.

Mrs. M. L. Polk, Phoenix, Arizona

RASPBERRY SALAD

2 c. red raspberries
Juice of 1 lemon
1 c. sugar

1 c. milk
1 c. whipped cream
1/2 c. chopped salted pecans

Rub raspberries through a sieve and measure 1 cup of the pulp. Add the lemon juice, sugar and milk to the pulp then fold in the whipped cream and pecans. Pour into freezer tray and freeze until firm, stirring once.

Mrs. Mildred Rivers, Charlotte, North Carolina

FROZEN SALAD LOAF

1 17-oz. can fruit cocktail
2 c. sour cream
3 c. miniature marshmallows

2 tbsp. fresh lemon juice
1/4 tsp. salt
Red food coloring

Drain the fruit cocktail and place 1/2 cup in bottom of 5-cup mold. Combine the sour cream, marshmallows, lemon juice, salt and enough food coloring to tint light pink. Add the remaining fruit cocktail and mix lightly. Spoon into mold over fruit. Freeze until firm. Unmold and cut into slices to serve. 8 servings.

Mrs. C. F. Clifton, Charleston, South Carolina

STRAWBERRY-PINEAPPLE CUPS

1 9-oz. can pineapple chunks
1 c. drained sliced strawberries
1 c. miniature marshmallows
1/4 c. broken pecans

1 env. unflavored gelatin
1/4 c. mayonnaise
1 c. heavy cream, whipped

Drain the pineapple and reserve the syrup. Combine pineapple, strawberries, marshmallows and pecans. Soften the gelatin in 3 tablespoons of the reserved syrup and heat the remaining syrup just to boiling. Add to gelatin and stir to dissolve, then add to the fruits. Fold the mayonnaise into the whipped cream, then fold into the fruit mixture. Fill paper baking cups with mixture and place in muffin pans. Freeze until firm. 16 servings.

Mrs. A. M. Sherman, Baton Rouge, Louisiana

STRAWBERRY-CHEESE SALAD

1 pt. strawberries	2 tsp. lemon juice
2 tbsp. sugar	1/2 c. whipped cream
2 3-oz. packages cream cheese	

Crush the strawberries with the sugar. Blend the cream cheese and lemon juice together until smooth, then stir in strawberries. Fold in the whipped cream. Place in mold and freeze.

Mrs. S. F. Barnes, Oklahoma City, Oklahoma

PIQUANT TOMATO SALAD

1 tbsp. unflavored gelatin	1 carton sour cream
2 c. tomato juice	1/8 tsp. dry mustard
1 sm. can crushed pineapple, drained	1/4 tsp. dry ginger
	Dash of red pepper
1/2 c. mayonnaise	1 tsp. onion juice
1 1/2 tsp. salt	Hot sauce to taste

Soften the gelatin in 1/4 cup cold water and dissolve in 1 cup hot tomato juice. Add the remaining tomato juice and remaining ingredients and mix well. Place in freezing trays and freeze until firm, stirring 3 times at 30-minute intervals to prevent flaking. 8 servings.

Mrs. H. C. Hammond, Paducah, Kentucky

FROZEN TUNA SALAD

2 tsp. unflavored gelatin	1 tsp. Worcestershire sauce
2/3 c. catsup	2 c. flaked tuna
2 tbsp. lemon juice	1 tsp. prepared mustard
3 tbsp. vinegar	1 tsp. prepared horseradish
1/2 c. mayonnaise or salad dressing	3/4 tsp. salt

Soften the gelatin in 2 tablespoons cold water, then dissolve over hot water. Add remaining ingredients and mix thoroughly. Spoon into a mold and freeze until firm. Unmold and slice. Serve on lettuce and garnish with tomato wedges and mayonnaise.

Mrs. A. T. Blackwell, Bentley, Louisiana

Souffle Salad (below)

SOUFFLE SALAD

2 c. boiling water	1 tsp. salt
2 3-oz. packages lemon	1 c. chopped celery
gelatin	1/2 c. chopped nuts
1 c. cold water	1/2 c. chopped dates
2 tbsp. lemon juice	Shredded lettuce
Mayonnaise	Strawberries

Pour the boiling water over gelatin in a bowl and stir until gelatin is completely dissolved. Add the cold water, lemon juice, 1 cup mayonnaise and salt and blend with rotary beater. Pour into a freezing tray or metal loaf pan. Freeze for 20 to 25 minutes or until firm about 1 inch from edge of pan but still soft in center. Turn into a bowl and whip with rotary beater until fluffy and thick. Fold in the celery, nuts and dates and pour into 9 x 9 x 2-inch pan. Freeze for about 1 hour or until firm. Unmold. Serve on lettuce and pipe mayonnaise rosettes on top. Garnish with strawberries. 8-12 servings.

FRESH PEACH SALAD

3 c. peeled and diced fresh	1/4 c. quartered maraschino cherries
peaches	1/2 tsp. almond extract
2 c. miniature marshmallows	1/8 tsp. salt
1/2 c. drained crushed pineapple	2 c. sour cream
1/2 c. slivered almonds	Few drops of red coloring

Combine all the ingredients in a large bowl and mix well. Pour into an 8-inch square pan or 12 muffin cups lined with paper baking cups. Cover with foil and freeze. Cut into squares or peel off paper cups before serving. 12 servings.

Mrs. B. B. Bland, Richmond, Virginia

WALNUT-CRANBERRY RIBBON LOAF

1   1-lb. can cranberry sauce
3/4 c. grated apple
1/2 pt. whipped cream
1/4 c. confectioners' sugar
1 tsp. vanilla
1/2 c. chopped English walnuts
  or pecans

Crush the cranberry sauce with a fork and stir in the apple. Pour into a freezing tray. Mix the whipped cream, sugar, vanilla and 1/3 cup walnuts. Spoon over the cranberry layer and sprinkle with remaining walnuts. Freeze until firm.

Mrs. H. V. Hill, Tampa, Florida

FROZEN PEAR SALAD

1 lge. can pears
1 pkg. lime gelatin
2   3-oz. packages cream cheese,
  cubed
Juice of 1/2 lemon
1/2 c. slivered almonds
1/2 pt. whipped cream

Drain the pears, reserving 1 3/4 cups juice. Bring the reserved pear juice to a boil and add the gelatin, stirring to dissolve. Add the cream cheese and lemon juice and mix well. Chill until thickened. Dice the pears and fold into the gelatin mixture with the almonds and whipped cream. Pour into a 9 x 9-inch pan and freeze, stirring once or twice.

Mrs. Ruth DeFriese, Knoxville, Tennessee

SUPREME FROZEN FRUIT SALAD

1 No. 2 1/2 can fruit cocktail
1 No. 303 can crushed pineapple
1   6-oz. package lime gelatin
2 1/2 c. miniature marshmallows
1 lge. can chilled evaporated
  milk, whipped

Drain the fruit cocktail and pineapple and reserve the juice. Bring reserved juice to a boil and add the gelatin and stir until gelatin is dissolved. Add the fruits and marshmallows, then fold in the whipped milk. Pour into individual molds or 1 large mold and freeze until firm. 20 servings.

Mrs. Jack Copeland, Tellico Plains, Tennessee

FROZEN ROQUEFORT AND CABBAGE SALAD

4 oz. Roquefort cheese
2 tbsp. cream cheese
1 tbsp. vinegar
1 tbsp. finely minced onion
1 tsp. paprika
1 c. whipped cream
1 c. finely shredded cabbage

Blend the Roquefort cheese, cream cheese, vinegar and onion together and add the paprika. Fold in the whipped cream and cabbage. Place in a refrigerator tray and freeze. Serve on lettuce and garnish with mayonnaise. 6 servings.

Mrs. Doris G. Grigsby, Lehigh Acres, Florida

Honey-Lime Dressing (page 176)

savory salad dressings

After the salad is prepared and ready to be served, the finishing touch must be added. That touch — as southern homemakers know — is the salad dressing. It must harmonize in flavor, texture, and seasonings with the salad ingredients. The right dressing can lift every salad to new heights of taste.

That's what this section is all about — it tells you how to select the right dressing for every salad recipe you'll find in this cookbook . . . how to prepare out-of-this-world homemade dressings . . . and how to individualize every dressing you serve with herbs and spices.

Echo the flavor of your fruit salad by serving Pineapple Dressing for Fruit Salad. Think what an unusual flavor combination you can offer your guests when you top your very best poultry salad with Cranberry Dressing. Offer southern versions of two Old World dressings by featuring Riviera French Dressing or Greek Salad Dressing as the finishing touch on your next salad. And you'll dazzle everyone's palate with your own mayonnaise — such as the Tangy Mayonnaise you'll find in this section.

These pages contain many more salad dressing recipes just made to bring out the best of every salad you serve. These dressing recipes are the home-proven favorites of *Southern Living* homemakers — and they're yours now to try — and to make your very own.

173

The finishing touch you add to your salad – whatever the type – is the dressing. There are dressings to match every salad you prepare. *French dressing* is a mixture of oil and vinegar, lemon juice, or wine, and your favorite seasonings. It may be clear or creamy. Clear dressings separate and should be well shaken before using – to thicken the oil and to mellow the vinegar, try adding an ice cube just before shaking. It works wonders! Creamy French dressings are homogenized and will not separate.

A covered glass jar is the perfect container for French dressing. Plan on a proportion of about four parts of oil to one part of vinegar – you'll have to experiment to find the exact proportion your family likes, but the four-to-one ratio is a good one to start with. There are many different kinds of oil available. Those most often used in preparing French dressing are olive, safflower, corn, or peanut. Olive oil by itself has a rather strong flavor . . .

general directions

SALAD DRESSINGS

and is expensive. Most homemakers find that two parts of vegetable oil mixed with one part olive oil keeps the flavor of olive oil from becoming overwhelming.

There are almost as many kinds of vinegar as there are salad oils. Red- and white-wine vinegars are economical to use and are not so acid as the cider vinegars. For flavor variety, you may want to have one of the herb vinegars on hand – tarragon is especially nice. And for extra-special dressings, try substituting dry sherry for vinegar.

Some cooks prefer to use lemon juice in place of vinegar in their French dressings. You may need more lemon juice than you did vinegar as the juice is less acid.

After you have mixed the vinegar and oil, add your seasonings. Thyme, marjoram, basil, parsley, chive, garlic, powdered mustard, or paprika are frequently used – you'll want to experiment to find your family's favorites. Two seasonings you're certain to want are pepper and salt. A homemade salad with your own special dressing deserves the flavor highlight of freshly ground pepper. Salt may be ordinary table salt . . . garlic salt . . . onion salt . . . seasoned salt – whatever you want to use to perk up the dressing.

One word of caution about herb blends: unless you are an experienced user of herbs, don't attempt to blend your own salad herbs. Most grocery stores sell herbs blended specifically for salads. These blends have been prepared by herb experts and contain just the right selection of herbs in the proper proportion to each other.

Mayonnaise is a creamy dressing made by adding oil – drop by drop – to egg yolks. Try making your own: it takes ten minutes (three if you've got a blender), and the difference in taste between homemade and manufactured mayonnaise is unbelievable. Mayonnaise may separate during the addition of oil. If this happens to you, begin again with another egg yolk. Add the oil very slowly until the yolk breaks down and mixes with the oil. When this takes place, use your first oil-egg mixture that had separated as you would oil. You'll have delicious mayonnaise without any wasted ingredients. The two secrets of successful mayonnaise are to add the oil drop by drop and to bring all ingredients to room temperature. And if you find the taste of mayonnaise made with olive oil too strong, try using a half-and-half blend of olive and vegetable oils.

Salad dressing, like mayonnaise, uses egg and oil. But the whole egg is used. In addition the salad dressing may depend on a starch for thickening.

Cooked dressings — also called boiled dressings — are high in egg content and low in fat. They are made by cooking an egg-based white sauce — and adding vinegar, fat, and seasonings to this base.

When time is short, you may have to forego homemade dressings for those you buy in the store. Try to find prepared dressings with the most basic blend of ingredients — the plain mayonnaise or salad dressing and the vinegar-and-oil dressing. You can add your own seasonings to these dressings — not quite the same as if you had made them yourself, but the next best thing!

If fruit or frozen salads are to be featured at your meal, try this hint for sparkling up your salad dressing. Save bits of canned fruit juices and syrups and use them to bring new flavor notes to the salad dressing you serve. Just mix a bit of the juice with the dressing at the last minute — imagine a pineapple-flavored salad dressing with a mixed fruit salad!

The chart below gives the calorie values of salad dressing ingredients and of prepared salad dressings you may find in your grocery store:

FATS AND OILS CALORIE CHART		
FAT OR OIL	**AMOUNT**	**CALORIE**
FATS, cooking (vegetable)	1 cup 1 tbsp.	1,770 110
LEMON OR LIME JUICE	1 tbsp.	5
MAYONNAISE	1 cup 1 tbsp.	1,450 110
OILS (salad or cooking)	1 cup 1 tbsp.	1,945 125
SALAD DRESSINGS: bleu cheese French home-cooked, boiled low-calorie mayonnaise-type Thousand Island	 1 tbsp. 1 tbsp. 1 tbsp. 1 tbsp. 1 tbsp. 1 tbsp.	 80 60 30 15 65 75
VINEGAR	1 tbsp.	2

HONEY-LIME DRESSING

1 6-oz. can frozen limeade concentrate	1/2 c. honey
3/4 c. salad oil	1/4 tsp. salt
	2 tsp. celery seed

Place the limeade, salad oil, honey and salt in a blender container and blend for several seconds. Stir in the celery seed. Mixture may be beaten or shaken to mix. Serve over fresh or canned fruit salad. 2 cups.

Photograph for this recipe on page 172.

ANSLEY DRESSING

2/3 c. sugar	1/3 c. honey
1 tsp. dry mustard	5 tbsp. tarragon vinegar
1 tsp. paprika	1 tbsp. lemon juice
1 tsp. celery seed	1 tsp. grated onion
1 tsp. poppy seed	1 c. salad oil
1/4 tsp. salt	

Combine first 6 ingredients in a bowl. Add the honey, vinegar, lemon juice and onion and mix well. Add the salad oil very slowly, beating constantly with electric beater at medium speed. Store in refrigerator in tightly covered jar. 2 cups.

Mrs. Joseph J. Shippen, Atlanta, Georgia

BLEU AND COTTAGE CHEESE SALAD DRESSING

1 c. cream-style cottage cheese	2 tbsp. chopped pimento
1/2 c. sour cream	2 tbsp. Worcestershire sauce
1/2 c. crumbled bleu cheese	1/4 tsp. salt
2 tbsp. minced onion	2 drops of hot sauce

Blend the cottage cheese and sour cream in a bowl. Mix remaining ingredients. Add to cottage cheese mixture and mix well. 2 cups.

Mrs. Mary L. Burleson, Swan Quarter, North Carolina

CHIFFONADE DRESSING

1/3 c. vinegar	1/2 tsp. dry mustard
1 c. corn oil	1 hard-cooked egg, chopped
1 clove of garlic	2 tbsp. chopped green pepper
1 1/2 tsp. salt	2 tbsp. chopped pimento
1 tsp. sugar	2 tsp. chopped parsley
1/2 tsp. paprika	

Combine all ingredients in a jar and cover. Shake well. Chill for several hours, then remove garlic. Shake well before serving.

Mrs. Carl Stephens, Nashville, Tennessee

CHUTNEY FRUIT DRESSING

3/4 c. powdered sugar	1 tsp. vinegar
1 tsp. paprika	2 tbsp. catsup
Salt and pepper to taste	1/2 c. salad oil
Juice of 1 lemon	1 tbsp. Worcestershire sauce
1/4 tsp. dry mustard	1/2 c. chutney

Place all ingredients in a pint jar and cover. Shake well. Store in refrigerator.

Frances Adams, Orlando, Florida

CITRUS PEANUT DRESSING

2 tbsp. orange juice	1/4 tsp. salt
1/4 c. peanut butter	1/2 c. sour cream
1/4 c. prepared mustard	1/4 tsp. grated orange peel

Blend the orange juice into peanut butter in a bowl gradually. Add the mustard, salt, sour cream and orange peel and refrigerate until chilled. Serve over fruit salads. 3/4 cup.

Mrs. Bob Williams, Camden, Arkansas

SWEET AND SOUR DRESSING

2 eggs	1 can sweetened condensed milk
3/4 c. vinegar	1/2 tsp. prepared mustard
2 to 3 tbsp. water	

Beat the eggs in a bowl until thick. Mix the vinegar and water. Add the vinegar mixture to eggs alternately with the milk, 1 tablespoon at a time, beating well after each addition. Blend in the mustard. Store in refrigerator in a tightly covered container. Serve on fruit salads.

Thelma Huff, Pelahatchie, Mississippi

SLAW SALAD DRESSING

1 c. vinegar	1/2 tsp. turmeric
1 c. sugar	1/2 tsp. salt
1 tsp. mustard seed	

Mix all ingredients in a saucepan and bring to a boil. Cook for 2 minutes. Cool, then refrigerate until chilled.

Mrs. William D. Varnell, Rogersville, Arkansas

Piquant Cherry Dressing (below)

PIQUANT CHERRY DRESSING

3/4 c. water	1/2 c. red maraschino cherry
1 tbsp. cornstarch	syrup
1/3 c. each frozen orange and	Dash of salt
pineapple juice concentrate	1 tsp. dried mint leaves

Stir the water into cornstarch in a saucepan gradually. Blend in the undiluted orange and pineapple concentrates, cherry syrup, salt and mint leaves. Bring to a boil over low heat, stirring constantly. Remove from heat and cool. Chill thoroughly before serving. One-third cup frozen orange or pineapple concentrate is about 1/2 of a 6-ounce can.

COOKED SALAD DRESSING

3 tbsp. butter or margarine	1/4 c. vinegar
3 tbsp. flour	1 tsp. salt
1 c. milk	1/4 tsp. mustard
2 eggs	1/8 tsp. paprika
1 tbsp. sugar	

Melt the butter in top of a double boiler and stir in the flour. Add the milk and cook, stirring, until thick. Beat the eggs slightly in a mixing bowl and add small amount of the white sauce, stirring constantly. Add to remaining white sauce. Add the sugar, vinegar, salt, mustard and paprika and place over boiling water. Cook for 5 to 10 minutes or until smooth and thick, stirring frequently. Remove from heat and cool. Store in covered container in refrigerator.

Dianne Woods, Chatham, Virginia

ARGYLE DRESSING

1 tsp. butter	4 egg yolks, beaten
1 tsp. salt	8 marshmallows, quartered
1 tbsp. sugar	1 c. whipped cream
1 tsp. dry mustard	1 c. chopped nuts (opt.)
4 tbsp. vinegar	

Cream the butter, salt and sugar in top of a double boiler. Dissolve the mustard in the vinegar and add the butter mixture. Add the egg yolks and mix well. Cook over boiling water until thick, stirring constantly. Add the marshmallows and stir until melted. Chill, then fold in the whipped cream and nuts.

Hazel S. Wilkinson, Ozark, Alabama

GINGER-CREAM DRESSING

1 c. pineapple juice	1 egg, well beaten
3 tbsp. lemon juice	1/2 c. miniature marshmallows
4 tsp. sugar	4 tbsp. finely chopped candied
1 tbsp. cornstarch	ginger
3/4 tsp. salt	1 c. cream, stiffly beaten

Mix first 5 ingredients in top of a double boiler and bring to boiling point, stirring constantly. Remove from heat and add to egg slowly, beating constantly. Return to top of double boiler and place over boiling water. Cook until thick, stirring frequently. Chill, then stir in the marshmallows and candied ginger. Fold in the whipped cream.

Mrs. Myrtle Menefee, Clint, Texas

PINEAPPLE DRESSING FOR FRUIT SALAD

1 tbsp. flour	1 egg yolk, beaten
Syrup from No. 2 can sliced	Dash of salt
pineapple	

Place the flour in the top of a double boiler and stir in the syrup gradually. Add the egg yolk and salt and mix well. Place over boiling water and cook, stirring constantly, until mixture coats spoon. Chill and serve on fruit salads. Do not use pineapple juice.

Mrs. Earl H. Martin, Hendersonville, North Carolina

IMPERIAL DRESSING

1/4 c. brown sugar	1/2 tsp. dill
1 1/2 tsp. salt	1/2 c. red wine vinegar
1/8 tsp. pepper	1 c. catsup
1 tsp. onion salt	1 c. olive oil
1/2 tsp. celery seed	3 tbsp. capers and juice
2 or 3 drops of hot sauce	1 tsp. Worcestershire sauce
1 tsp. paprika	1 clove of garlic, minced

Combine the sugar, salt, pepper, onion salt, celery seed, hot sauce, paprika, dill and vinegar in a saucepan and bring to a boil. Cool for 10 minutes. Blend in the catsup, olive oil, capers and Worcestershire sauce. Add the garlic and cool for 1 hour. Place in a jar and cover. Refrigerate until chilled. Shake well before using. 2 3/4 cups.

Mrs. Nancy Armstrong, Oklahoma City, Oklahoma

SPINACH DRESSING

1 egg	1/4 c. vinegar
1 tbsp. ham drippings	4 tbsp. sugar
4 tbsp. sour cream	

Beat the egg in a saucepan. Add remaining ingredients and heat through, stirring constantly. Do not boil. Serve over spinach and garnish with hard-cooked egg slices.

Mrs. J. A. Cleek, Chattanooga, Tennessee

CRANBERRY DRESSING

1 c. jellied cranberry sauce	2 tbsp. lime or lemon juice
1 c. mayonnaise	1 c. whipped cream (opt.)

Blend the cranberry sauce and mayonnaise in a bowl with electric mixer. Add lime juice and beat well. Fold in whipped cream and chill.

Mrs. Mary Blandford, Atlanta, Georgia

DILL DRESSING

1 tbsp. dillseed	Pepper to taste
1 1/2 tsp. dry mustard	2 tbsp. tarragon vinegar
1 tsp. salt	6 tbsp. salad oil
1 tbsp. sugar	

Mash the dillseed well in a bowl. Add the mustard, salt, sugar and pepper and mix thoroughly. Add the vinegar and stir until sugar is dissolved. Add the oil and stir well. 6 servings.

Mrs. John W. White, Albuquerque, New Mexico

DATE SALAD DRESSING

2 eggs
1/4 c. lemon juice
1/4 c. sugar

1/8 tsp. salt
1 c. whipping cream
1 c. chopped dates

Beat the eggs in top of double boiler and blend in the lemon juice, sugar and salt. Cook over boiling water, stirring constantly, until thickened. Remove from heat and cool. Whip the cream until stiff and fold in egg mixture and dates. Serve over fruit salads. 3 cups.

Mrs. Winston Cross, Richmond, Virginia

FRENCH DRESSING

2 tbsp. Basic Dry Mix
1/4 c. vinegar

3/4 c. corn oil

Place the Basic Dry Mix, vinegar and corn oil in a jar and cover tightly. Shake well.

Basic Dry Mix

3/4 c. sugar
1/4 c. salt

4 tsp. paprika
4 tsp. dry mustard

Mix the sugar, salt, paprika and mustard. Store in a tightly covered jar.

French Dressing (above)

CELERY SEED FRENCH DRESSING

1/2 c. sugar
1 tsp. dry mustard
1 tsp. salt
1/2 sm. onion, grated

6 tbsp. vinegar
1 c. salad oil
1 tbsp. celery seed

Combine the sugar, mustard, salt, onion and half the vinegar in a bowl. Add oil gradually, beating constantly, then beat in remaining vinegar. Add the celery seed and mix well. 1 1/2 cups.

Mrs. W. M. Piersall, Tarpon Springs, Florida

FRENCH DRESSING

3 tbsp. sugar
3 tbsp. catsup
1 tsp. salt
1/2 tsp. dry mustard

1/4 c. evaporated milk
1/2 c. salad oil
3 tbsp. vinegar

Combine all ingredients except vinegar in a bowl and beat until well blended. Add the vinegar and beat thoroughly. 1 1/4 cups.

Mrs. Margaret W. Lyles, Westminster, South Carolina

RIVIERA FRENCH DRESSING

1/2 c. salad oil
1 tsp. salt
1/2 tsp. pepper
1/4 c. vinegar
3/4 tsp. powdered sugar

1 thin slice onion
2 sprigs of parsley
1 whole pimento
1 1/4-in. strip green hot
  pepper

Place all ingredients in blender container and cover. Blend thoroughly. 1 cup.

Mrs. Beulah Gibson, Athens, Alabama

GREEK SALAD DRESSING

3/4 c. olive oil
1/4 c. red wine vinegar
1/8 tsp. dry mustard

1/2 tsp. salt
1/4 tsp. pepper

Place all ingredients in small jar and cover. Shake thoroughly and chill before serving. 6-8 servings.

Mrs. Pat Fisher, Houston, Texas

TANGY LIME DRESSING

3 tbsp. fresh lime juice
3 tbsp. honey

6 tbsp. salad oil

Combine all the ingredients in small mixing bowl and beat at medium speed with electric mixer until thoroughly mixed. Serve on fruit salads.

Mrs. W. E. Hill, Tulsa, Oklahoma

LIME-MINT DRESSING

3/4 c. salad oil
1/4 c. lime juice
1 tsp. salt
1/4 tsp. white pepper

1 tsp. finely chopped parsley
1 tsp. finely chopped mint
1 tsp. finely chopped chives
1 tsp. prepared mustard

Combine all ingredients and add 1 ice cube. Beat until mixture thickens. Serve on tossed green salad or coleslaw.

Sandra England, Centertown, Kentucky

LOW-CALORIE THOUSAND ISLAND DRESSING

1 c. low-calorie cottage cheese
1/3 c. catsup or chili sauce
1 tbsp. lemon juice or vinegar
2 hard-cooked eggs, chopped

2 tbsp. drained chopped dill
   pickle
Salt and white pepper to taste

Blend the cottage cheese in a blender until smooth. Add remaining ingredients and mix well. 4-6 servings.

Mrs. Annie Potts, Moss Point, Mississippi

FRUIT MAYONNAISE

1 tsp. butter
2 tsp. flour
1 1/2 c. pineapple or grapefruit
   juice
Juice of 1 lemon

Juice of 1 orange
1/2 c. sugar
2 eggs, separated
1/2 c. heavy cream, whipped

Melt the butter and blend in the flour. Add the fruit juices and sugar and cook over medium heat, stirring constantly, until thickened. Pour over the beaten egg yolks slowly, stirring vigorously. Cool. Fold in the stiffly beaten egg whites and whipped cream. Chill and serve over salads.

Grace Strutt, Bessemer City, North Carolina

TANGY MAYONNAISE

1/4 tsp. paprika	2 tbsp. vinegar
Dash of cayenne pepper	2 c. corn oil
1 tsp. salt	2 tbsp. lemon juice
1/2 tsp. dry mustard	1 tbsp. hot water
2 egg yolks, at room temperature	

Combine the dry ingredients and blend in the egg yolks. Add the vinegar and mix well. Add 1 teaspoon of the oil at a time, beating at high speed until 1/4 cup has been added. Add remaining oil in increasing amounts, alternating last 1/2 cup with lemon juice. Beat in the hot water. 1 pint.

Barbara Waybourn, Afton, Texas

BLENDER MAYONNAISE

1 c. salad oil	1/2 tsp. salt
1 tbsp. vinegar	1/8 tsp. paprika
1 tbsp. lemon juice	1/4 tsp. dry mustard
1 egg	Dash of cayenne pepper

Pour 1/4 cup of the oil into electric blender and add the vinegar, lemon juice, egg and seasonings. Cover and blend for 5 seconds. Remove cover, while blender is running, and add remaining oil in steady stream. Turn off blender immediately after adding oil. 1 1/2 cups.

Josephine L. Grissette, Montgomery, Alabama

CUCUMBER DRESSING

3 med. cucumbers	1/4 tsp. garlic powder
3 sm. onions	2 tbsp. Worcestershire sauce
1/4 c. sugar	1/4 tsp. green food coloring
1/4 c. lemon juice	1 qt. mayonnaise
1/4 tsp. monosodium glutamate	

Grind the cucumbers and onions and drain well. Place in a bowl. Add the sugar, lemon juice, monosodium glutamate, garlic powder, Worcestershire sauce, food coloring and mayonnaise and stir until smooth.

Helen Hutchison, Jackson, Tennessee

CRAB LOUIS DRESSING

1 c. mayonnaise	1/4 c. chopped green onion
1/4 c. sour cream	1 tsp. lemon juice
1/4 c. chili sauce	Salt to taste

Combine the mayonnaise, sour cream, chili sauce, green onion, lemon juice and salt in a bowl and mix well. Chill. 2 cups.

Dorothy Blake, Wheeling, West Virginia

FLUFFY CELERY SEED DRESSING

1 8-oz. package softened cream cheese	3 tbsp. water
1/4 tsp. garlic salt	1/2 c. instant nonfat dry milk
1 tsp. Worcestershire sauce	1 tsp. celery seed

Place the cream cheese, garlic salt and Worcestershire sauce in a 1 1/2-quart bowl. Beat with electric mixer at low speed until smooth, adding water gradually. Beat at medium speed for about 1 minute, adding the dry milk and celery seed gradually. Chill. About 1 1/3 cups.

Fluffy Honey Dressing

1 8-oz. package softened cream cheese	1/4 c. honey
	1/2 c. instant nonfat dry milk

Place the cream cheese in a 1 1/2-quart bowl. Beat with mixer at low speed, adding honey gradually. Beat at medium speed for about 1 minute, adding the dry milk gradually. Chill. 1 3/4 cups.

Fluffy Lime Salad Dressing

1 8-oz. package softened cream cheese	1/4 c. water
2 tbsp. lime juice	1/2 c. instant nonfat dry milk
	1 tsp. grated lime rind

Place the cream cheese in a 1 1/2-quart bowl and beat in the lime juice and water with electric mixer at low speed until smooth. Beat at medium speed for about 1 minute, adding dry milk and lime rind gradually. Chill. 1 1/2 cups.

Fluffy Salad Dressings (above)

Piquant Ripe Olive Dressing (below)

PIQUANT RIPE OLIVE DRESSING

1 1/4 c. honey	1/4 tsp. celery salt
1/2 c. cider vinegar	1 1/2 c. canned pitted ripe
1/2 c. salad oil	olives
1/4 tsp. salt	

Beat the honey in a bowl until frothy, then stir in the vinegar, oil, salt and celery salt gradually. Slice the olives and stir into dressing. 3 cups.

ICE CREAM SALAD DRESSING

4 tbsp. vanilla ice cream	2 tbsp. crunchy peanut butter
2 tbsp. mayonnaise	Pineapple juice

Mix first 3 ingredients in a bowl and stir in enough pineapple juice to thin to desired consistency. Serve over fruit salads.

Mrs. R. D. Bowling, Mobile, Alabama

PLANTATION SALAD DRESSING

1 pt. mayonnaise	1 clove of garlic, crushed
1/2 pt. French dressing	2 tbsp. anchovy paste
3/4 c. grated Parmesan cheese	

Combine all ingredients in a bowl and cover. Store in refrigerator. Serve on lettuce, if desired.

Mrs. Craig Selden, Tucson, Arizona

ROQUEFORT-CURRY SALAD DRESSING

2 c. mayonnaise
1/2 lb. Roquefort cheese,
   crumbled

1/2 tsp. curry powder

Combine all ingredients in a bowl and mix well. Cover and refrigerate until chilled.

Mrs. Clyde Hester, Baton Rouge, Louisiana

SEAFOOD SALAD DRESSING

2 c. mayonnaise
1/4 c. catsup
1/4 c. chopped green onions
1/4 c. chopped dill pickles
2 hard-cooked eggs, chopped

1/2 tsp. pepper
1 clove of garlic
1 can shrimp
1 can crab meat

Mix the mayonnaise and catsup in a bowl and stir in the onions, pickles, eggs and pepper. Add the garlic and cover. Place in refrigerator for several hours. Remove garlic. Drain and chop the shrimp. Drain the crab meat. Fold shrimp and crab meat into dressing.

Mrs. Evelyn H. Duke, Columbia, Louisiana

SPRING GARDEN DRESSING

1/2 c. mayonnaise
1/2 c. cottage cheese
3 tbsp. chopped green pepper

1 tsp. salt
Dash of pepper

Combine all ingredients in a bowl and cover. Chill.

Ena Mae Jenkins, Elizabethtown, North Carolina

RUM-CREAM DRESSING

1 3-oz. package cream cheese
2 tbsp. sugar
1 tbsp. rum
1 tbsp. lemon juice

1/4 tsp. grated lemon rind
Dash of salt
1/2 c. whipped cream

Blend the cream cheese and sugar in a bowl. Add rum, lemon juice, lemon rind and salt and blend until smooth. Fold in the whipped cream. Serve on fruit salads. 1 cup.

Wanda Baker, Atlanta, Georgia

SWEET MUSTARD DRESSING

1 c. mayonnaise	1/4 c. sugar
1/4 c. mustard	1/4 med. onion, grated

Combine the mayonnaise, mustard and sugar in a bowl. Add the onion and mix well. Refrigerate until chilled.

Esther H. Collier, Evergreen, North Carolina

LEMON SALAD DRESSING

1/2 tsp. grated lemon peel	1/2 c. cottage cheese
Juice of 2 lemons	1 tbsp. sugar
1 lge. banana, sliced	

Combine all ingredients in a blender container and cover. Blend at low speed for 30 seconds. Blend at high speed until smooth and creamy. May be thinned with a small amount of milk, if desired. 1 1/4 cups.

Mrs. Byron James, Jackson, Mississippi

WATERCRESS SALAD DRESSING

2 eggs	1 tsp. salt
2 c. salad oil	1/3 c. vinegar
2 tbsp. horseradish	2 tbsp. paprika
1/4 c. catsup	1 tsp. Worcestershire sauce
2 tbsp. grated onion	Dash of hot sauce

Place all ingredients in a quart jar and cover. Shake vigorously. Refrigerate until chilled. Serve over watercress and top with chopped onion and crumbled bacon, if desired.

Mrs. John G. Zierdt, Redstone Arsenal, Alabama

MAYFAIR DRESSING

1 tbsp. pepper	4 tbsp. horseradish mustard
1 tbsp. monosodium glutamate	1 stalk celery, chopped
3 eggs	1/2 med. onion, minced
1 tbsp. anchovy paste	2 c. salad oil

Place all the ingredients except the oil in a blender and blend well. Add the oil, 1/4 cup at a time. Pour into a 1-quart jar. Keeps for 2 weeks in refrigerator. 1 quart dressing.

Mrs. James M. Howarton, Las Vegas, Nevada

PHOTOGRAPHY CREDITS: Planter's Peanut Oil; Olive Administrative Committee; Planter's Peanuts; California Avocado Advisory Board; Washington State Apple Commission; United Fresh Fruit and Vegetable Association; Florida Citrus Commission; McIlhenny Company; Tuna Research Foundation; National Broiler Council; Pickle Packers International; National Macaroni Institute; North American Blueberry Council; Cling Peach Advisory Board; Best Foods: A Division of Corn Products Company, International; Rice Council; U. S. Department of Commerce: National Marine Fisheries Service; California Raisin Advisory Board; Armour and Company; National Livestock and Meat Board; Sunkist Growers; Pineapple Growers Association; International Shrimp Council; American Dry Milk Institute, Incorporated; The R. T. French Company; Diamond Walnut Growers, Incorporated; Spanish Green Olive Commission; National Cherry Growers and Industries Foundation; General Foods Kitchens: Good Seasons Onion Salad Mix; Keith Thomas Company; Campbell Soup Company; National Dairy Council; California Dried Fig Advisory Board; Pet, Incorporated; American Honey Institute.

Printed in the United States of America.